Contents

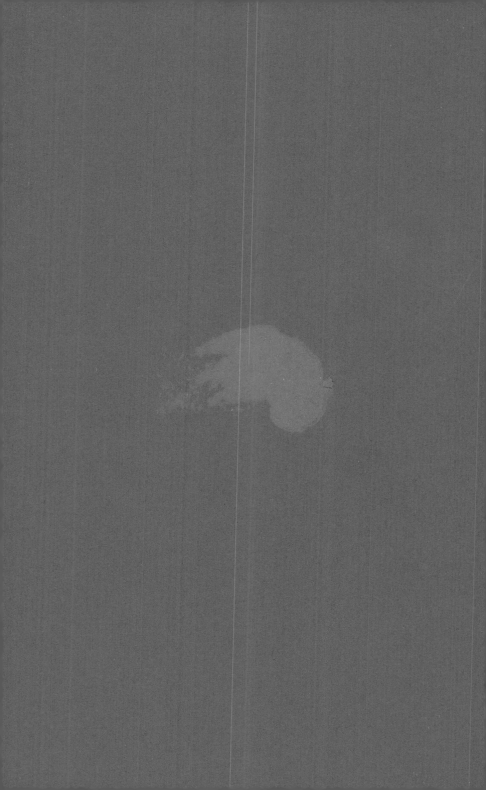

TOM DIAPER'S LOGBOOK

Captain Tom Diaper

TOM DIAPER'S LOGBOOK

MEMOIRS OF A RACING SKIPPER

CAPTAIN TOM DIAPER

ADLARD COLES NAUTICAL

BLOOMSBURY

LONDON · OXFORD · NEW YORK · NEW DELHI · SYDNEY

*I Dedicate This Book
To My Grand Daughter
Doreen
For her kindness to me*

Adlard Coles Nautical
An imprint of Bloomsbury Publishing Plc

50 Bedford Square   1385 Broadway
London   New York
WC1B 3DP   NY 10018
UK   USA

www.bloomsbury.com
www.adlardcoles.com

ADLARD COLES, ADLARD COLES NAUTICAL and the Buoy logo are trademarks
of Bloomsbury Publishing Plc

First published 1950 as *Tom Diaper's Log* by Robert Ross & Co., Ltd.
This edition published 2016

British Library Cataloguing-in-Publication Data
A catalogue record for this book is available from the British Library.

Library of Congress Cataloguing-in-Publication data has been applied for.

ISBN: HB: 978-1-4729-3080-4
ePDF: 978-1-4729-3082-8
ePub: 978-1-4729-3081-1

2 4 6 8 10 9 7 5 3 1

Typeset in Joanna MT Std by Deanta Global Publishing Services, Chennai, India
Printed and bound in Great Britain by CPI Group (UK) Ltd, Croydon CR0 4YY

MIX
Paper from
responsible sources
FSC® C020471

To find out more about our authors and books visit www.bloomsbury.com.
Here you will find extracts, author interviews, details of forthcoming
events and the option to sign up for our newsletters.

Foreword

Sailing, as I have done, on the big classic yachts that race in high-profile venues around the globe, it has been impossible not to be impressed by the high level of seamanship required to operate these craft. Today, many of them are power-assisted with inboard engines, modern winches, electronics and even computer-driven, hydraulic sail trimming. No such benefits were around in Tom Diaper's day. Piloting was by 'Lead, Log, Lookout and Trust-in-the-Lord', while deck work was all 'Armstrong's Patent', horny fists and a lifetime of learning how to throw what weight you had in the right direction.

Crews in the third millennium are often well educated. Most carry some sort of official qualification and the deckhand who has not spent time on sophisticated training courses is now the exception rather than the rule. The relationship of the fo'c's'le and the owner's party has moved a galactic distance from a world when, skippers perhaps excepted, the men forward of the mast were hired, fired and barely noticed by many of 'the quality' in the saloon.

When Tom Diaper and his shipmates raced against the Kaiser, and Sir Thomas Lipton's giant gaff cutters were competing for the America's Cup, the crew were hard-bitten professionals of working-class stock. Most were Essex fishermen who had left school before their voices broke. A few, like Tom Diaper, hailed from a similar background in and around Southampton. Pay was poor, but prize money helped and there was always the chance of a good bonus when they won a race on which their owner had staked a large sum.

Tom Diaper's Logbook leaves no doubt about the sheer scale of the mighty yachts in the so-called 'big class', but he also reminds us of humbler jobs, sometimes equally satisfying in the end. However, his pithy observations on *Shamrock IV*'s failure to lift the great prize from the Americans are priceless, shining a bright light on a foredeck perspective we would be hard-pressed to find elsewhere. Penned many years after the event, they are undiluted by tact, political correctness, or any concerns about upsetting his employer. Indeed, the forthright nature of this unique account from an unlettered man of the old school has to be required reading for social historians as well as yachting enthusiasts. That his family have preserved the log and seen to its publication stands to their eternal credit. Those of us who yearn for deeper insights into the Golden Age of Yachting are in their debt, as we are to a publisher with the vision to deliver this new imprint to our cabin tables.

The words of the log echo down to us on the gales of time. Whatever ethereal seas he is sailing now, we wish Tom Diaper and all the hands of his generation fair winds, eased sheets and a snug berth when the great race is run.

Tom Cunliffe
2016

Introduction to the 1950 edition

The first sight of Captain Tom Diaper's memoirs was rather depressing. A bundle of pages torn out of an old exercise book, each one filled to bursting-point with a solid mass of close writing in a large, sprawling and somewhat tremulous hand; no chapters or paragraphs; spelling decidedly eccentric and apparently fortuitous. However, the script was legible and I dipped into it, hardly expecting to be rewarded for my pains. Very soon I found myself wondering what the old man was going to say next and I read on and on till, with eyes aching from the strain of deciphering the script and the clock pointing to long after my normal bed-time, I came to the end and realised that I had been completely carried away by this unsophisticated, but vivid and convincing narrative.

Then I began to wonder why I, a man with no special interest in yachts and no previous acquaintance with the author, should have been so fascinated by his stories. True, he has had many interesting experiences and has come across a few notable personalities – particularly the late lamented Kaiser Wilhelm. But that was not what kept me out of my bed. It was not the Kaiser who interested me so much as Captain Tom Diaper's reactions to the Emperor and his entourage. Thinking it over, I realised that I had been attracted by the extremely vivid picture that the author gives of himself; and Captain Tom Diaper is undoubtedly a character. Brave, competent, self-reliant and at times self-assertive; he holds his head high, knows his own value and will suffer no one to trample on him. Not unduly elated by success, he keeps his chin up in adversity and one feels the pathos of his repeated disappointments in his search for a permanent job – a job that would give him such security as is possible in his rather hazardous calling.

Moreover, Tom Diaper has somehow learned to use words in a simple and effective way. They are not the words of a professional writer and his syntax is decidedly irregular, but he writes as he talks: lucidly, emphatically, and to the point. The spelling has been rendered more orthodox, but the syntax seemed to be so much part of the story-teller that it has been left to add its rich colour to the background. Here and there a slight obscurity has been removed, but only so as to involve the least possible interference with the original words. The narrative has been paragraphed and divided into chapters and a few short passages have been cut out, but in other respects it reaches the reader almost in the same shape as was given to it by that ancient mariner, Captain Tom Diaper.

It is not often that a simple old man is allowed to tell the story of an adventurous life in his own words. Too often his manuscript is handed over to a hack writer, who 'improves' it with padding, decorates it with fictitious descriptions and dilutes it with a liberal admixture of clichés, so that the result is almost indistinguishable from the typical products of second-rate journalism.

Diaper is not a professional author. He has spent almost all his life on the sea and has told the story of that life in the language of the forecastle. That story has been passed on to the public in its authentic form. Readers who like their literary fare to be correct and colourless are advised to put this book back on to the shelves and choose something else. However, anyone who enjoys a good story told with force and character in rough but effective language can turn to Tom Diaper with joyful anticipation. And if the reader happens to be interested in yachts and their racing, his pleasure will be so much the greater.

Sidney Wadsworth
1950

Introduction to this edition

Tom Diaper was born in Itchen Ferry Village, a thriving fishing and ferry community on the banks of the river Itchen near Southampton. The Itchen Ferrymen were so prized for their maritime skills that whole families made their livelihoods as merchant seamen and yachtsmen. The village was small, with just a few families who for centuries had combined running the ferry and fishing with being farmers and yeomen; like many insular communities they developed local crafts and culture particularly connected to the water: rope making, net craft, boat building and silk work.

The village was centred on Peartree Green, where legend has it Queen Elizabeth I planted the pear tree that gave the green its name. The green looked out over the river to the town of Southampton and the ribbon of red-brick houses built near the church and school led down to the ferry and the older ferrymen's cottages, and of course to long-standing pubs such as the Yacht and the Royal Oak. The Itchen ferry fishing boat was also used for local sailing and rowing races, and boat builders, such as Dan Hatcher, developed the design to create the proper racing yachts that had become a favourite pastime of millionaires such as Sir Thomas Lipton as well as royalty such as Edward VII and the German Kaiser.

It was into the sailing families such as the Diapers, the Parkers, the Jurds and the Dibles that Tom Diaper was born. His father and grandfather were both successful yacht captains and all of his brothers also went to sea, often crewing for their brother Alfred, who was the favourite skipper of Sir Thomas Lipton on his famous *Shamrock* America's Cup yachts. Tom was unusual in that he wrote a memoir of his life at sea. The book is cherished by his descendants and inspired an exhibition and the founding of the Diaper Heritage Association. The family tree has 10,000 entries and traces the family back to the time of the Norman Conquest. More information on the history of Itchen Ferry Village can be found on the website www.diaperheritage.com.

This new edition of the book has had some of the minor mistakes from the original edition corrected, as well as the addition of endnotes (thanks to Martin Black), designed to inform the reader about the yachts and ships mentioned, as well as various people and occasions Tom discusses. Some additional photos from the family have also been included, as well as dates in the margin to clarify the year it is that Tom is talking about. We hope this new edition of the Log will inspire others to research their family history and to find out more about the lives of pioneering yachtsmen.

The Diaper Heritage Association
2016

1
The Diapers of Itchen

When. The Sail was set and it bellowed out to the Breeze one of the Sailors said now that is The Sail To make her Spin a gentleman on board Took it from That Phrase and reversed it Called it Spinmaker Eventually Shortening it To The name of Spinnaker

At a very early time I can remember events in my life. My father was a sailor, fisherman and yacht captain, born in the village of Itchen opposite Southampton with the river Itchen running between. His name was Thomas Diaper[1], known to all he was acquainted with as Tommy 'Dutch' Diaper – it is the same as I am called at times. We come of a long line of fishermen, sailors and, in early days, noted smugglers inside the Isle of Wight and especially at Netley, Hythe and Itchen. One gentleman who owned the 40-ton racing yacht *Norman*[2], a Major William Ewing, traced our ancestors back to the landing of William the Conqueror at Hastings. The yacht *Norman* was that in which my father made his name as a good racing skipper.

My mother's maiden name was Lonnon. That was another name of note in the village, but the Lonnons were not so numerous as the Diapers. There was ten children in our family, four girls and six boys, a girl being born first. Then comes myself born on the 20th August, 1867, bringing my age to 82

An original Itchen Ferry boat

this coming August. All my five brothers took to the water, all being yachtsmen.

The first yacht my father took skipper of was the famous racing
1863 yacht *Niobe*[3]. He was serving in a yacht called *Destiny*[4], when his father, who was at that time skipper of *Niobe*, died, and my father was asked to take his place. His age was then 25, and the *Niobe* was the first yacht to set a spinnaker[5].

A Mr Gordon was the inventor at the time. He owned the business of sailmaker at the bottom of High Street, Southampton, and my grandfather was the skipper. They took the yacht out to the English Channel and set and tried the spinnaker. There have been many who have asked why the sail was named spinnaker. This is how it was told to me by my father.

When the sail was set and it billowed out to the breeze, one of the sailors said, 'Now that is the sail to make her spin!' A gentleman on board took that phrase and reversed it to spinmaker, eventually shortening it to spinnaker, and so it is called today. All this is as it was told to me; I am open to correction.

Now the first yacht of which I have recollection of being aboard was the racing cutter yacht *Christabel*[6]. I cannot tell the owner's name, but my father was skipper. She laid up for the winter at Cowes, and he had to look after her. The owner gave him permission to have his wife and children to live on board for the winter, and that was the first I remember. There was a gentleman who used to come on board wearing one of the old-fashioned flat straw hats, yellow straw inside, and black shiny outside, just as though it had been painted with black enamel, and he always had a large black dog, and a walking stick with rather a large crook to it. I do not remember his name, but I do remember these things about him. He was the owner of the yard. Once when the yacht was laid up for the winter, my sister who was about four years and six months old (I was two years younger) was nursing my   1870
brother who was about four–six months old, and she let him fall. His face touched the stove which was very hot, burning it, and leaving a scar which he carried for years. My father said my memory of this was true, too[7].

After that I do not remember much, only school, till I was the age of six, then two events occurred that are in my memory. One was that I entered the village church choir, and the other was the midsummer holidays from school began. My father took me on the yacht *Norman*, of which he was skipper at that time. I raced   1873

3

Tom's father, Tommy 'Dutch' Diaper

on board of her that year in every race she ran inside the Isle of Wight and continued to do so every year till I was 14 years of age. The *Norman* had held the record of her Class. Other yachts were built against her that year, they were longer and carried more sail – the *Sleuth Hound*[8] and the *Annasona*[9] – the latter being the crack boat. After the Solent races were finished, to get a few prizes the *Norman* parted from her Class. She went over to France, my father taking me with him. That was the last time I saw the owner. The

1881

4

Norman returned to England and was laid up at Gosport, and I was on board until she finished laying up and was put in the market for sale.

My father's next yacht was the Sleuth Hound of the same Class. I left school then, and in January the following year I started my proper sea-going days. My father got me a berth as pantry boy on board the steam yacht Queen of Palmyra[10]. Leaving Southampton in March, 1882, the yacht was chartered by a Mr Cross of London from the owner, the Marquis of Exeter.

1882

* * *

I remember the first trip well for there was another boy on board; he shipped as cook's boy. After we had passed the Needles there was a strong wind east, and a bit of a sea running. The sailors set the squaresail and the trysails, and the wind freshened as we proceeded. We had the deck full of coal in sacks to make sure we had enough to take us to Gibraltar; myself and the other boy was very seasick, and we lay completely done-in on the coal sacks on the after part of the ship. About 5pm when we had the Start Point abeam, the first mate came and told us it was time for us to go and turn in. We both slept in the forecastle in one wide bunk. We started to go forward and the cook's boy said he wanted to be sick again. He leaned over the side to do so, and I continued on forward. I had just reached the deckhouse forward when the cry of 'Man overboard' rang out. The second mate was at the wheel steering the ship – he was the father of the cook's boy. The first mate pushed me in the deckhouse and told me to stay there. All was in a hustle then, taking in sail and rounding the ship to search for the boy who, I learned, had over-reached himself and had toppled into the sea. Someone had thrown a lifebuoy, but the last that was seen of the boy he was swimming for the

Documentation and crew list for the Queen of Palmyra,
dated 1st March 1882.

log-line that was over the stern. We searched about for two hours but never caught a glimpse of him, so we had to give him up as lost. It put a sad gloom over us all, and all pitied his father. The boy was very winning and I can tell you I cried and missed him awfully, as he was my bedmate. We proceeded on as we could do nothing else, but we talked only about his loss, wondering if a large sailing fishing smack had picked him up, and why the old man (meaning the skipper) had not waited to speak to her. Being only a boy I could not understand much[11].

There was one more incident. When the first mate put me in the deckhouse it was littered with straw where the stewards had been unpacking stores. Now as they turned the ship round she rolled very much in the heavy sea that was running. The blue signal lights was in a rack in the deckhouse, and one of them must have got dislodged. It must have fallen nose-downwards and ignited when it struck the floor. I had the presence of mind to pick it up, open the door and throw it into the sea. Then I found that the straw was on fire and getting a good hold. With good luck I trampled it out, and did not think any more about it. I did not think anyone had seen it, all hands but myself being busy reducing sail and looking for the boy, but the day after when the men was talking about the loss of the boy, one of the crew asked if anyone had seen a blue light go over the side, seeming to come from the deckhouse. No one else had seen it; but the steward coming in to ask me if I could turn out (as I was very seasick still and in my bunk) enquired if I knew what all that burnt straw meant in the deckhouse. Then it come to my memory about the blue light and the fire. So I had to go and tell my tale to the skipper, who strongly praised my presence of mind on such an occasion, saying it might have stopped a serious fire, everybody being so busy on deck doing their duty trying to save the boy. This was my first bad thrill at sea. It cast a dead gloom over the ship.

7

Nothing else of note occurred on the way out to Gibraltar, which was reached in seven days eight hours. We laid there replenishing our stores and taking in coal and water. The captain shipped a Maltese boy in the place of the poor cook's boy what was lost. From Gibraltar we proceeded to Nice, took in the charterer and friends and proceeded to cruise about the Mediterranean. We stayed a long time at Naples, and it was then I saw the ruins of Pompeii, the ladies taking me with them to see it. I saw a lot of queer sights; one of them was the mummy of a baker and the oven where they found 80 loaves. I had to stop with the ladies, the gentlemen going by themselves. I have not been to Pompeii since, but I hear they are still clearing away the ashes and lava. Two days after I went with the ladies to see the Blue Grotto on the Island of Capri. They call it the Blue Grotto because the water is perfectly blue inside. We rowed in our boats while the yacht waited outside. Inside there were several Italian boys in boats who earn a lot of money by people throwing money into the water for which they dive in. They nearly always get it before it gets to the bottom – if there is a bottom! I have not heard, or have forgotten whether the boys prefer silver coins, but of course they have greater value and are easier to see. It is a queer sight to see the boys under water – they are naked, and show up pale blue while the water is a darker blue.

From Capri we went on to Malta. The Maltese boy and myself went on shore together. He showed me the cathedral where the golden gates were taken or stolen from. It was at this port that the captain got a severe talking to and had to go before some high officials ashore for not reporting at Gibraltar the loss overboard of the cook's boy, which I have since learnt should have been done at the first port the yacht touched after the loss occurred. I do not know exactly how the officials found out, but the Maltese boy, being a native of the place, talked a lot about it ashore, and they may have heard, made enquiries and found out that it was true. Anyhow, the skipper was severely reprimanded, which I think he deserved.

There are what they call 'bumboats' at Malta, boats that bring all kinds of curios for sale. I bought several things to take home to my mother and sisters. You can purchase some fine lace there. Now while we was there an incident happened that I should think brought all the people in the Island to Malta. There was a large fleet of all kinds of warships there, and the day they left it was a grand sight. The battleship *Alexandra*[12] led the way out amid thunderous cheering from the people ashore, and all ships blowing their whistles, for they were starting on their way to bombard Alexandria; the Egyptian war was on. I have talked about that event several times since to my brother-in-law (that is now) for he happened to be in that war, in the Royal Engineers, and was mentioned in dispatches.

We went from Malta to Algiers and Tunis on the African coast; from there we went over to Genoa on the Italian coast and worked our way back to Gibraltar. From there we called in at Vigo, but we struck a rock at the entrance; so when we arrived at the harbour we had a diver down to see what damage had been done. He found that we had knocked off about 30 feet of our keel. It was wood – I forgot to mention that the *Queen of Palmyra* was a wooden ship. The damage was not so bad, and we was allowed to proceed on our way. We left there and had a very good crossing of the Bay of Biscay, arrived at Torbay and anchored at Torquay on the coast of Devon on the 20th August, 1882. It being my 13th birthday, the ladies gave me strawberries and cream and a large cake for tea.

From Torquay we went direct to Southampton, and landed the gentry as the charter was up. The captain put me ashore for a week's leave, and the yacht proceeded to Cowes, laying up at

Marvin's Yard, West Cowes. All the crew was paid off with the exception of the first mate and myself. I can tell you I felt a bit of a man when I walked home to see my parents, carrying 100 oranges and several curios. I met my former school-mates and seemed to have grown more than them. I rejoined my ship at the end of the week. The crew were recalled by the owner, the Marquis of Exeter, who had her fitted out for the remainder of that summer. He was Commodore of the Royal Victoria Yacht Club, Ryde.

We visited the Channel Islands, did some fishing there and returned to Cowes where we laid the yacht up again at Marvin's Yard. All the crew was paid off except the first mate and myself. I was kept on her for a couple of months and then paid off as they could not get a charter for her. I remember that pay-off, for I had shipped at eight shillings a week and my keep. I had arranged for four shillings a week to be left at Payne's Yard, Southampton[13], for my mother, but I found when I got home that they had not drawn a penny of it, so my father and mother took me with them to draw it. Then they took me to a jeweller's and bought me a watch and chain with the half pay I had left for them to use. I could not thank them enough and thought how kind it was of them. So I ended my first voyage working for my own living.

2
Deck Boy and Steward

Then Able seamen were very Strict on the Boys at meal times the boys had to Stand back. the men Taking Their Share. first. after them the Ordanory. Seamen. Took Theirs then came the boys. to help Them self to what was left. Sometimes I can tell you they had a Very poor share

It was only a little while before I shipped in a Union Cape cargo boat called the *Asiatic*[1], signing on as deck boy. A deck boy's life at that time was pretty hard. We used to be on all day, and turned in all night. We turned out at 4am and had coffee and biscuits. There was no soft bread for us; for dinner we had salt pork and peas and salt beef and potatoes every other day, biscuits and butter for tea and breakfast, and only boiled rice and molasses for Saturday's dinner. We had no fresh meat after three days out until reaching Cape Town. Then on the African coast we had beef and spuds or mutton. The able seamen were very strict on the boys at meal times, the boys had to stand back, the men taking their share first. After them the ordinary seamen took theirs, then came the boys to help themselves to what was left. Sometimes, I can tell you, they had a pretty poor share.

After we went on deck at 4.30am our first job was to go round with a bucket of sand and water and a piece of rough canvas to sand-and-canvas all the ladders and steps which was bare wood, whilst the men in the Watch washed down the decks. It was winter and dark and cold; sand-and-canvassing was not a pleasant job. After that we had to clean all the brass work. There were only two deck boys, myself and one other. Every two hours, starting at 6am and finishing at 8pm, with two ordinary seamen and the quarter-master, we had to go aft and heave the log. This was a large reel with a long line reeled on it. Two boys or two ordinary seamen used to hold the reel on the end of which was a piece of wood with a three-piece line attached. One end of the three-piece had a wooden plug fastened into a hole in one corner of the triangular piece. A boy held a sand glass. When the wood on the end of the line was put over the side and the quartermaster let the distance line run through his hand and came to the distance mark on the line, he said 'Turn!' Then the boy with the sand glass turned the glass upside down, and when he said 'Stop!' that was when the last grain of sand had passed through the small neck of the glass from the top to the bottom half. Then the quarter-master and the rest grabbed the line and the jerk caused the wooden plug to come out of the triangle piece and release one of the lines in its corners so that you could haul in easier, the wood being end on. The line was marked at intervals, and the nearest mark in the quarter-master's hand when the boy called out 'Stop!' notified the speed the ship was going by the number of marks on the line which had passed through the quarter-master's hands. So that was how I learned what heaving the log was.

1883   We were gone six months on this voyage. Having half-loaded the ship with bales of wool and hides at Algoa Bay, the order came to tranship it to another company's ship, and to prepare our ship to stop on the African coast to relieve the other coast-boat. We laid in Algoa Bay some time and I had a very good time. I used to go out with the captain in the dinghy sailing about the bay. When the captain did not want me or the dinghy, I went with the officers fishing on the Roman Rock out in the bay. I remember that well, for on the last time we anchored by the rock a bird called 'the diver' came close to the boat. The fourth officer was putting the bait on his hook when he suddenly threw the lead at the bird. One of the hooks caught his finger and the hook broke. It left a jag in his finger and we could not get it out. So we finished fishing and rowed and sailed back to the ship. I helped to hold the fourth officer while the doctor cut the hook out of his finger.

The next day we had orders to load up again for England, the order being that a smaller vessel was taking the place of coast-boat. When we were loaded we proceeded to Cape Town, filled up there with coal and stores and left for England. On the way home the captain asked me to come on the next voyage and said he would raise me to ordinary seaman. In them days you did not have to serve three years as deck boy or ordinary, but was promoted on one's conduct and ability, so I suppose he thought I was capable of taking the job. But I told him I would let him know when we paid off. The captain and officers had taken a great liking to me. The first officer offered to learn me navigation, but the yachting life was more to my liking.

We reached Southampton one day in the late spring, and we had to wait until the next day to be paid off. In the morning of that day I was asked to go as messroom steward of the Steam Yacht *Dobhran*[2] of about 500 tons, belonging to Mr T Valentine Smith of the book and paper stalls in the railway stations. So I shipped there for the summer. I went and thanked the captain of my last vessel, the *Asiatic*, for all his kindness to me, also the officers, who said they were sorry to lose me. They offered that if ever I wanted a ship or a helping hand I should go and see them, but the captain died soon after.

Well, I put in that summer in the *Dobhran*, going to Loch Aline in Scotland in September, and staying there till the end of October. We then returned to Southampton, moored the yacht off the town quay and all hands were paid off. I had a holiday for a month, then I shipped as boatswain's boy in the Cape Union ship *Athenian*[3]. I made three voyages to the Cape in that ship that winter. We had some good sports in her on the voyages. I won the obstacle race on all three voyages. One voyage I won £9 prize money, and a gentleman who had been yachting with my father gave me £2. He told me that he had backed me against a crack steward to the amount of £20. I won all the obstacle races in every ship in that company what I had entered in.

The following summer I heard that the *Dobhran* wanted a second steward and I tried for the job, but I was too late. So I went fishing in my father's boat for that season, my father being out of a job.

The following winter my father was asked to take charge
1884 of a Southampton racing yacht called *Marguerite*[4], building at Lymington, and the builders gave him the job to fit all the rigging, so I went with him as his mate. That was where I gained a lot of experience in the way of splicing wire, etc, and the way to rig up a yacht when the yacht had finished building. I went in her as steward, my age being about 15. We did not have much of a summer in her, only winning two first prizes and nothing else. She proved a failure. All hands was paid off including my father and myself. Another captain was appointed to her for the next summer but he did not do any better in her. The following
1885 winter I made three voyages to the Cape in the *Athenian*. After the next summer my father was unlucky at getting a job in England, but an American gentleman offered him to go over there and take charge of a 40-ton racing yacht *Ileen*[5], so he went and took me

with him as AB. I was rather young for that position, but still I had
a lot of experience for my age.

We made a good summer over there, but the owner got
married at the end of the year and did not fit out the yacht
again. Of course to get over there the owner paid all our fares,
second class, both going and coming. The next season my father
was offered the skipper's job on a 10-tonner, but he would not   1886
accept it so passed it on to my cousin who took the job and I went
with him as cook-steward and deck-hand combined. The owner
was a brother to the owner of the 40-tonner *Ileen*. He bought
the 10-ton racing yacht *Ulidia*[6] in England at Brightlingsea. We
took her to London and shipped her on one of the Hill Line
cattle ships. The yacht was of the narrow type of those days
with very much draught. They put her on deck in a large cradle
and built us a cabin on the cattle deck. It took us four days to
get to New York, having very heavy weather. When they put the
yacht in the water a tow-boat took us in tow and towed us to
Tomkinsville, where they put us in the Seawanaka Yacht Club
Basin on Staten Island. There we fitted her out after going for
a few sails in New York Bay. We went through Hell's Gates to
New Rochelle; there we sailed our first race, and won the first
prize. We went from there to New London, where we beat our
opponent again[7]. We raced in all 12 times that year, going to
Newport, Rhode Island and down to Bar Harbor, Maine. At Bar
Harbor we had a very heavy gale, all other yachts slipping their
moorings and going to a place for shelter called Salem. But we
stayed on, running ropes to three different moorings, the gale
died down and we had a quiet night. We laid the yacht up at
the end of the summer and returned to England in the Cunard
steamer *Servia*[8].

And that following winter I made three voyages to Cape Town
in the *Athenian* as ordinary seaman. I did not stay out of work long.

1887 After I finished again in the *Athenian* in the early spring, I again shipped in the 10-ton *Ulidia* and went to Staten Island, USA, to join her.

* * *

1887 That summer we had a new boat against us, she was a centreboarder, very wide and very shallow. We beat her seven times out of 12, the other five she won in light weather, but we could beat her in a breeze. It was the year that the *Thistle*[9] went to America to bring the Challenge Cup away, but she did not do it. She threw the chance away. Now before that race took place, our owner and the owner of our opponent was at the Seawanaka Yacht Club. They challenged one another and put down £100 a side to sail their yachts around Long Island, the winner to take the £200. Our owner told us that if we won we should have the whole of the stake to share amongst us. We shipped up three more hands for the race, that making a double crew, the other boat doing same. The start was to be at New Rochelle in Long Island Sound, and the finish to be off Seawanaka Yacht Club, the distance being about 250 miles. This was a long race, for if there should happen to be a strong breeze outside the Island, we should make bad weather of it. We started at 12 noon one Friday with spinnakers for the run down Long Island Sound. The wind was very light which suited the other boat. It was a strong breeze we wanted and windward work, but the luck seemed dead out for us, for as we reached the turning point of the Island, the wind followed around with us, so we carried spinnaker and bowsprit spinnaker all the way around, till we entered New York Bay and to within ten minutes of the finishing mark. Then the wind came too late for us. If we had had that breeze all the way around we should have beaten her, but she beat us by an hour[10]. Hard luck

16

on us, but the owner paid us £2 for every 24 hours. We started at 12 noon on Friday, then finished at 6pm on the Sunday evening, making 54 hours. I will leave you to guess what fine weather it was. I cooked for all the people on board all the way around, and had good hot meals all the time. It was bad luck for us we lost that race. The owner left us as soon as we finished and told us we could invite a few friends and finish up all drink and eatables what was left and have a good night of it. We did not that night, but turned in and had a good night's rest instead. But next night we kept to his word and had a good party.

Now before all this happened a gentleman guest on board asked us three in crew if we would like to stop in America. All three of us said we would, but as the time came for us to finish laying the yacht up for the winter, the other two said they would not stop in America. I followed suit and went home with them in the Cunard Steamer Etruria[11].

The following winter I again made three trips to the Cape as able seaman. The spring came round again and I shipped in the famous racing cutter 90-ton Irex[12], owned by Mr John Jameson. Captain W O'Neill was the skipper, and we raced all around the coast, winning a good many prizes. That year we beat all records in the races inside the Isle of Wight and made a clean record in the race around the Island[13]. After the racing was over we went cruising over to the Channel Islands, and from there we went to the Scilly Islands fishing, Mr Willie Jameson being on board. They hired a fishing boat and crew. The boat used to go out in the evening and set the long lines leaving them down all night, then the next morning we would sail out in the yacht as close as we could get and the gig's crew would take Mr Jameson and guest in the gig to the fishing boat and watch the fishermen haul the long lines. It was there I saw the largest conger I ever saw. It weighed 90 pounds and they had a hard job to land it in the boats. It

1888

barked very much like a dog. We stayed at the Islands two weeks catching many fish, large cod and skate besides large plaice, etc, then we returned to Southampton laying the yacht up at Fay's Yacht Yard, paying all hands off in the fall. The following winter I 1888/9 went fishing myself in my father's boat.

'I shipped in the famous racing cutter *Irex*'. © Beken of Cowes.

3
Father and Son

he had only just been married he had a kind of a what-not made arround the foormast to put all his wedding presants. a funny place to put them has I told him with the work of the mast and ship there was very soon a leak and salt water & fresh. when it rained poured through on to these presants which was mostly silver and copper

The next summer I again shipped in the *Irex*, my father taking charge of the first *Valkyrie*[1], 70 tons, owned by the Earl of Dunraven. She was in our class, and beat us more times than we beat her. We went to all the same places as the year before, starting the race first at Harwich.

1889

I remember one instance when we beat all the rest of the class easy. That was on the Clyde; it was all reaching, starting at Hunters Quay and finishing there. We was finished and I had just unshackled the jib halyards. A passenger steamer had just passed by, the *Valkyrie* was cheering us and Captain O'Neill called for all hands to answer her. The steamer's wash was making us roll terrible. Now the jib halyards was of chain and it was as much as I could do to hold on to the block and chain halyards, so I could not go to the side of the deck where the rest of the crew was giving the *Valkyrie's* answering cheer. Captain O'Neill looked round the mast and saw me. The words he said was, 'Oh! I see you do not cheer when we win, but only when your father wins in the *Valkyrie*.'[2]

Pure spite, I thought, for a captain to say that to a lad, for I was only 22 years of age then. So I thought I would answer him back. The words I said to him was, 'Well, captain, don't you think that a pound winning money is just as good in my pocket or better for myself than in the pocket of the *Valkyrie's* crew?' Well, things had not been very good for me that summer. I could do nothing right, whereas the summer before I could do nothing wrong. I put it down then and there that the cause of my doing nothing right was my father beating him more times with the *Valkyrie* than any yacht since Captain O'Neill had been in the *Irex*. By some people O'Neill was reckoned the crack skipper of the day, but a good many did not think so. He may have been a good man, but where there is one good man there are others. I do not think he would have done so well with the *Irex*, had it not been for Mr Willie Jameson[3] and the second mate, Ben Parker. They two had most of the steering while I was there and before I was there, I was told.

I have always found the result of a race lay mostly to the man that steers the boats, just the same as a jockey with a horse, but be the helmsman ever so good, he cannot get a boat along if it is not in the boat. Now with a racing yacht a captain depends largely on luck, or what I call luck, in the design of the boat he has the chance to get skipper of. I will take two boats both 40-tonners and two skippers. The skippers their names was Captain Willie O'Neill and Captain Willie Sherman, the yachts was *Annasona* and *Sleuth Hound*, the former's skipper was O'Neill, the latter's Sherman. The yachts was designed and built side by side by Willie Fife, the *Annasona* was, I am told, built off the inside lines of the *Sleuth Hound*. The former proved what you may calls a 'flyer,' taking a lot of prizes, whilst the *Sleuth Hound* was only getting a prize or two, and that was when it blew what you might call a gale of wind. Hence the result was that O'Neill was called a crack skipper and Sherman had to leave the *Sleuth Hound*. If they had changed ships before they started, the crack name might have been given to Sherman. I know for sure that Sherman had to leave, and his name practically disappeared as a racing skipper, for my father was given charge of the *Sleuth Hound* the next summer.

Now to return to my own: the same evening of the occurence with Captain O'Neill and myself at Hunter's Quay, I went on board the *Valkyrie* and asked my father if he would give me a passage home, as I intended leaving the *Irex*, but he persuaded me to hang on till the end of the season. But after the Clyde and the Irish Coast races was finished we left for Southampton, and on the way I could still do nothing right for the skipper. So when we arrived at Southampton I gave 24 hours' notice. I had a hard job to get my money. I got it after waiting three weeks for it.

When the racing started, the fortnight inside the Isle of Wight, I went as extra hand in a 20-ton racer called the *Mimosa*[4], then when I finished there I shipped as AB in the Union Castle boat *Nubia*[5] making three trips to the Continent and South Africa. The next summer I shipped with my father in the first *Valkyrie*, I was second masthead man[6] and bowsprit man. I was only in her till nearly the end of the season. Lord Dunraven, the owner, had a 5-ton racing yacht. I was bow-man of the gig and we was anchored at Calshot Castle as the 5-tonner *Alwida*[7] was going to race there that day. I was in the gig waiting to take Lord Dunraven on board the 5-tonner. My father called me out of the gig and told me I was to get in racing rig as I was to race in the 5-tonner. I naturally thought I was only an extra as the skipper of the 5-tonner was home ill, but on arriving on board, Lord Dunraven called me aft

1890

TOM DIAPER'S LOGBOOK

and asked me if I understood a stopwatch and knew anything about the Brambles[8]. When I told him I did, he said I was to get him a good start and keep the yacht afloat and see if we could win a prize. I was lucky enough to get the start and kept the lead the whole race and took first prize. When we finished we heard the skipper of her was dead. Then Lord Dunraven came and asked me to become skipper of the 'five,' which I did. We raced 12 races and took ten first prizes, and Dunraven was very pleased with me, putting me on a retainer for the winter, and free to go anywhere I liked as long as I was back in time for the next season. But all this was very soon altered. I was to draw the retainer once a month. I had the first month's retainer all right. A week after this my father had a 12 months' money sent him and was told he was not wanted on the *Valkyrie* any longer. My father asked Lord Dunraven the reason for this, and was told that the designer, GL Watson, could not agree as to who should fit the *Valkyrie* out for the next season, Watson saying he should do it. My father told Watson he might be able to design a yacht, but my father as skipper was the man who was to sail her. He should be the one to fit the rigging of her gear for sailing and then he would know what strain he could put on the gear so as not to carry away anything, and so he could see that everything was strong enough. But as Watson wanted to do all this and my father would not agree to it, Lord Dunraven parted with my father with much regret. So practically speaking that was the last time my father took charge of a racing yacht in England[9].

* * *

A week after this I received my second month's retainer and was told that I was not wanted on the 5-tonner any more. I suppose the thought was to get rid of the father and then the son, which

22

they did. My father had taken the Yacht Tavern, a public house in the village of Itchen, and had a fishing boat about 22 feet long, so I went fishing that winter and my father stayed and looked after his business. Although him and myself tried for several berths in yachts, no one would employ us. Anyhow, I managed next season to ship in a 20-tonner called the Mischief[10] and owned by a Naval Lieutenant who was a surveyor of life-boats around the coast of Ireland and Wales[11]. After fitting out I was cook-steward and deck-hand and I can tell you I had my hands full. We had to go to Kingstown, Ireland, to pick the owner up with his wife. He had only just been married, and he had a kind of a what-not made around the foremast to put all his wedding presents. A funny place to put them, as I told him. With the work of the mast and ship there was very soon a leak and salt water and fresh water, when it rained, poured through on to these presents, which was mostly silver and copper, and it took some of my time to keep them clean.

1891

As soon as the owner arrived on board at Kingstown he made that place his starting point for testing life-boats. His time was 12 o'clock noon fixed for the test. After testing the Kingstown life-boat he would send a telegram to the next place to tell them to be prepared for the test the next day at 12 noon. A funny thing to do in a sailing yacht. We would then get under weigh and sail for the next life-boat station. Now this was when I began to get dissatisfied after cooking three meals for us a day. There was three of us, skipper, one deck-hand and myself, I being the cook-steward. I had to cook breakfast, lunch and a 9 o'clock dinner for the owner and his wife. By the time I was through with the washing up, it was generally 11pm to 11.30pm. Then as we was sailing through the night, I had to go on deck at 12 midnight and take two hours steering the boat and one hour on the lookout, so by the time we got to the north of Ireland, carrying on like this day and night, I was fed up, and the weather changing from moderate to rough, the owner decided to return to Kingstown and visit the life-boat stations on the west coast by train. So when we got back to Kingstown I gave 48 hours' notice, having sent home for money to pay my passage home. The owner said he was sorry I was going, but I left and went from Kingstown to Dublin and took passage on one of the North Wales boats to Holyhead.

Now I was sitting in the forepart of the boat waiting for her to leave when a passenger came and spoke to me, and says he, 'If I get drunk, or seasick, would you see that I get on the Manchester part of the train at Holyhead?' I told him I would, so he asked me to go to the bar and have a drink. So seeing that he had had several drinks before and the boat having left, I went with him and had one drink with him. I was dressed at the time in a peak cap, reefer jacket and blue jersey, with *Valkyrie* in yellow letters across my chest. There was three others at the bar, and who I found out afterwards was in a habit of crossing often and of a very rough character. Whilst myself and my new friend was chatting, one of the others came and asked me for the loan of a pocket knife, if I had one, to cut up a pipe of tobacco. After he had done so, he put the knife in his pocket and walked away, so I followed and asked him for my knife. He turned round and said he had not got it, and, seeing that I looked like a sailor, could I tell him the name of the point of land we was passing?

I said I did not know, all I wanted was my knife. My friend had followed me up close; he had an Irish blackthorn stick in his hand. The fellow what had my knife, said he had not had it. My friend said that if he did not hand the knife over, he would crack his skull with his blackthorn, and as to me being a sailor I was no such thing; 'But bedad, can't you see?' says he, 'That he is a railway porter and the name on his chest is the name of the railway station he comes from.' Whereupon they all three

Tom and his wife Fanny at the time of their wedding, 1890

set about us. There was a rough and tumble for a few minutes till some of the ship's officers came and stopped it, ordering the other three fellows on deck, taking their names and saying they would never be taken passengers on that boat any more. It was not the first time they had caused a disturbance on that ship. The officers then told us they were noted pickpockets and card sharpers. When I reached Holyhead and I was seeing my friend to his part of the train, he pulled out a stocking and he told me there was £200 in it and he was going to Manchester for two months' holiday, and he would like me to go with him and help him spend it. But I would not, so I parted from him and went to my part of the train, as I wanted to get home to my wife, for I had only been married a twelvemonth. I forgot to mention it before. I

1890   got married on the 7th November[12], as I was finished in the *Alwida*, Dunraven's 5-tonner.

4
Navahoe versus *Britannia*

*Satanita either had to sink
a large passenger boat with about
30. persons. on board which
had suddenly appeared around
the stern of a yacht at anchor.
So keeping clear of her he the
Captn of the ~~Sand~~ Satanita could
not keep clear of Valkyrie II
So he colided with her cutting
the Valkyrie to the water*

I got home from the Mischief the next day and in the evening one of the crew of the Maid Marion[1], a 60-ton racing yacht, came to my home and said his captain would like to see me the next day. So, of course, the next day I saw him and shipped up in her as AB and bowsprit man. You got a shilling a week more than the other ABs. Only them that help such positions as masthead man, bowsprit man, and man looking after the gig or cutter had a shilling a day extra more than the rest.

I stayed in the Maid Marion that season winning several prizes[2]. When we laid up at the end of the season I was out of work a month. There was no such thing as insurances in those days. If you was out of work and you had not saved any money, you got nothing and you could not borrow, for everyone was placed the same. Anyhow after the month I shipped in a small steam yacht which Lord Egmont had chartered for the benefit of his health, as he was ordered to take daily trips on the water. He lived at an hotel in Alverstoke, near Gosport. I shipped as cook-steward. We was stationed at Stoke Bay to be handy for him to come on board. One day he invited the Admiral of Portsmouth to have a trip and lunch on board. Lord Egmont asked me to see what I could do in the way of a good lunch. Anyhow we steamed about and let go anchor at Cowes to have lunch quietly, and after it was over, the Admiral and Lord Egmont asked me where I had learned my stewarding and cooking, as the lunch was excellent. I can tell you I was a bit proud of myself and he very often after that invited people for a trip and lunch on account of that, so he said. I stayed in her till the charter was up in the spring, then I rejoined

1892 the Maid Marion as masthead man for that summer. We took a lot of prizes.

After we laid the Maid Marion for the winter and all hands paid off, I went and done my yearly month's drill on board the training ship Trincomalee[3], moored off Southampton Quay, for I had joined the First Class Royal Naval Reserve that summer at Dover. It was a very cold winter that followed. After I done my month's drill I shipped as AB in the Union boat Scot[4] and made three trips to South Africa and back, each trip taking six or seven weeks. In the

1893 following spring I reshipped again in the Maid Marion in my old position as masthead man. But as the summer advanced towards August and we did not race very many times I left her and shipped as extra under my father aboard the American yacht Navahoe[5], in which my father had shipped as pilot for the remainder of the season.

Racing in England, the Navahoe was in the large class with the Britannia[6], Valkyrie II[7], Satanita[8], Calluna[9] and Irex. The Navahoe had Jack Barr as a captain, but he was sent home shortly after we had started racing, my father becoming captain and pilot of her until McCarrol (the owner) had sent to America for another captain.

Navahoe and *Valkyrie* at Cowes, 1893. © Beken of Cowes.

Here I would like to mention something that occurred between my father and a well-known yacht owner, myself being present at the time. It was this way: we met this gentleman one day and he asked my father if it was true that he had shipped in an American yacht. My father said it was true, and what was the reason why he should ask him that question?

'Why,' the gentleman said, 'It is this way with you, that if you take pilot of that American yacht, you, Tommy, will never get another job as skipper of an English yacht again.'

'Well,' my father answered, 'As to that, I have shipped in her and shall go in her. For,' he said, 'I cannot get a skipper's job in an English yacht now. Why did not any English yacht-owner think of that before? As no one has thought of me lately and I cannot get my living in an English yacht I must get my living somewhere, even if it is under an American flag, and my son Tom also.'

'Well,' the gentleman answered, 'If that is the way, you must look out for yourselves. For we will swamp you, for there will be six English yachts to one American.'

'Well,' my father answered, 'Let you all try. You will not catch me napping, as you know you cannot if there was a dozen of you!' And he proved his word in not being caught napping, but the English gentleman also proved his word about the English yacht, for my father never took charge of an English yacht for years after, myself also included.

We had a good many races with the class, and close races they were too, the six English yachts trying all they knew how to jam us between them; but on the whole I think the Navahoe proved a little too fast for them, for we generally finished first, second or third. We also raced for the Breton Reef and the Cape May Cup against the Britannia; we lost the race at the east end of the Isle of Wight owing to a mishap to a our bowsprit whisker.

Now a curious thing happened when we raced from the Needles, round Cherbourg breakwater and back[10]. We were racing under American racing rules. At the starting line, between the Needles and a tug-boat moored about half a mile west of that, there was a strong wind east, and each yacht had a double reefed mainsail; the start was at 12 noon. We in the Navahoe allowed the Britannia to cross the line one minute and 18 seconds ahead of us, so that by the American rule, she would have to allow us one minute and 19 seconds over the line at the finish of the race, to take the prize away from us or retain it. For it was the Genesta[11] and Galatea[12] that brought the Breton Reef and Cape May Cups over from America.

It was an exciting race between us. First the Britannia was ahead of us, then we would overhaul her and pass her and keep ahead of

'We also raced against the *Britannia*'.

her. Then she would do the same. We went in at the west end of the
Cherbourg breakwater neck and neck and we came out of the east
end with a slight lead. There was a nasty sea and more wind, both
of us lowering our staysails. We continued on our way back across
the Channel in the same way, first one yacht taking the lead and
then the other. On nearing the Needles and the finishing line the
Britannia had a slight lead; we were close astern and yawing about
in the heavy sea that was running at the time. Both vessels having
set their staysails, Captain Hank Haff sent me forward to assist the
mate and to see that we did not touch the *Britannia*, so close were
we when we crossed the line of the Needles. We hauled our staysail
down and sailed in easy. There was no gun and afterwards we
found there was no committee boat, but when we reached Alum

Bay, we saw her anchored there. Afterwards we found out that the weather being so bad and the sea so rough and not expecting us back so soon, she had put in there for shelter. We continued up the Solent and moored off Cowes for the rest of the night.

When we turned out the following morning we saw that the Britannia had the winning flag up. Our owner would not have ours put up and would not go on shore to see about who had won out of the two of us. So all the crew and the extra hand mustered together and told him that no one on board would sail in another race if he did not see into it, as by the American rule we had won the race fair and square. So he went on shore and the committee settled it that we had won the prize and not the Britannia. The Britannia hauled her winning flag down and we pulled our first prize up[13].

As we had won it, I continued in the Navahoe all the remainder of the season, taking pilot of her in several races, as my father went home sick for a week and I took his place. After that my father came back and we went down the west, racing at Weymouth, Torquay and Dartmouth. After Dartmouth we brought the Navahoe up to Southampton, put her in dry dock, and before she returned to America, I stood by her till she left.

I shipped in the UMS Scot again as able seaman, making three voyages to the Cape and down the coast as far as Durban. One voyage – we anchored outside in them days, and put our cargo into lighters which were towed out of the harbour – this voyage it came on to blow very hard and we got under weigh and steamed up and down the coast till it moderated enough to anchor, and the lighters could come out and take the remainder of our cargo.

* * *

After we arrived at Southampton and was paid off, I started to look about for a yacht for the summer again. I shipped as mate under

Capt Ned Matthews in a 20-ton racing yacht designed by Watson,   1894
and built at Gourock on the Clyde, Scotland, for a German named
Graf von Douglas or Count Douglas, who, I learned after, was a
descendant of the family what was called the 'Black Douglases'
who had to get out of Scotland years before. This one settled
in the Baltic on an island called Rugen, or rather this one was
descended from the one what had to fly from Scotland. Now this
yacht was called Ellen[14] and was so far behind in her building that
we was too late for any races, so we had to get to the owner's
place on the Isle of Rugen as soon as we could. We went from
Gourock round to Cowes to pick up some sails what Ratsey had
made for us, and we called at Southampton to see our wives and
families before we started on our voyage to the Baltic. We had a
couple of days with them and then left.

We arrived at the Isle of Rugen. We had on board four German
deck-hands and a Scot cook, one of the Germans being a native
of Rugen. A fisherman piloted us through the narrow entrance
to the Inland Sea, as it was uncharted. It was a fairly large sea
with plenty of room for a long day's cruise, but before we
started cruising the skipper and myself sounded and buoyed
all dangerous points and shoals and made a chart of the Inland
Sea. After we had done this, the owner had all the German deck
hands on shore and to work in his park and garden, and while
they worked in the garden they had to leave the yacht's uniform
on board and wear their own clothes to work in the garden, and
when they came on board for a sail they had to wear the yacht's
uniform. We only went out of the Inland Sea on one cruise down
the Baltic, then we went to Sassnitz; from there to Travemünde,
down as far as Swinemünde[15]. After getting back to Rugen,
off the village, what was called Bergen, the owner wanted the
Germans to work in the garden again, but this time they refused;
so they all packed in and left[16]. So there we were with only a

skipper, mate and cook for a crew and when we did go out for a sail, we took as extras a gardener and coachman, until such times as we could get another crew, which I was doubtful whether we would get under the conditions of sailor and gardener combined in one. Anyhow, after trying all the villages around the Inland Sea of Rugen I came across a man what had been a sailor. He was working on a railway at the time and he told me all the wages he received was nine marks a week, about the worth of our nine shillings. And he had to keep 13 children and a wife out of that and what he did with a boat and net at fishing. The only food they lived on was fish, potatoes and black bread. As for meat, they very seldom saw that, and when they did have any, they had caught a good catch of fish and sold them to get the meat for a change. Anyway he shipped with us at the rate of 18 marks a week. That was the pay at the time for a German yacht AB, restricted by the Kaiserlich Yacht Club. There were very few yachts in Germany at that time. We cruised about in the *Ellen* till the middle of October; then it began to get very cold and started to freeze. So we took the *Ellen* to a place called Stralsund[17] and laid her up for the winter.

Now there is one thing I would like to mention here. It was while we was fitting the *Ellen* out at Gourock; it was the Clyde Fortnight Regatta; the large yachts were racing at Hunter's Quay. The American yacht *Vigilant*[18] – my father was pilot of her all the time – was racing on this side of the Atlantic with the *Satanita, Britannia* and *Valkyrie*. It was 5th July and I had the day off, so I walked from Gourock to the Cloch Lighthouse to witness the start of the race. It was in the start of this race that I saw the *Satanita* sink the *Valkyrie*. It was a bad thing, but I was too far away to see the actual cause of it, but as I was told by a closer eyewitness, it was a forced collision. The *Satanita* had to avoid a large passenger boat with about 30 persons on board, which had suddenly appeared around the stern of a yacht at anchor. In keeping clear of her he, the captain of the *Satanita*, could not keep clear of *Valkyrie II*, so he collided with her, cutting the *Valkyrie* to the water, while he knocked his own bow right off. He managed to keep the *Satanita* afloat but the *Valkyrie II* sank. All this happened whilst I was watching from the Cloch Lighthouse opposite[19]. This was while I was fitting out *Ellen*. After we laid the *Ellen* up at Stralsund we were all paid off and me who was mate, the skipper and Scotch cook returned home.

5
Trooping to Bombay

*Now you should have seen
The state of the troop decks for
with nearly 2000 troops being
Battened down for they could
fling their Hammocks up in that
storm and laid about any.
where and all or nearly all
Sea sick.*

After I had a month's holiday I joined the troopship *Victoria*[1] at Southampton to take troops out to Bombay, India. I was the only Southampton able seaman on board, the rest were mainly Cockney sailors. We left Southampton with the Enniskillen Regiment, and various drafts of other regiments, making a complement of 2,400, including a lot of women and children. When we arrived off Ushant Point, to enter the Bay of Biscay, we ran into a hurricane of wind with mountainous seas. I was in the starboard watch and below at the time. We were suddenly called out to secure grog. On the troop deck were some dozen barrels which had broken down the temporary building they were stored in, and while we were trying to secure them the order came for all hands on deck to repair steering gear, for we had smashed the stern steering gear. We had three steering wheels aft under the poop, so six of us took hold of them whilst the carpenter tried to lock it, but he could not have properly locked it, for after we had straightened her up on her course, she gave one heavy plunge and broke the lot of hand steering gear.

1894/5

So there we was at the mercy of the hurricane, rolling one side in and out, for being a single-screw ship the captain could not manoeuvre her to get her head to sea, the same as you could a twin-screw boat. So there we was drifting broadside on to the wind and mountainous seas, and for 53 hours not one on board had any cooked food. For the ship rolled so much the cooks could not keep their feet, or a pot on the stove, let alone cook any food. Each of us sailors had to go to the first-class bar and have a drop of brandy and a biscuit and cheese, for we were kept busy trying to catch the quadrant and we were breaking all our warps we could put on it. At last we got our 8-inch steel towing hawser. After we got this up out of the fore-hold we passed both ends aft, one on each side of the ship. Previous to this we had 400 of the best troops up on deck, all the rest being battened down, 200 stationed on each side to help us with the wire. The fourth officer and myself was working side by side. Sometimes him and sometimes myself was called away to try and secure a boat which was in danger of being torn from the davits and, as him and me told one another, it was the only time that we had ever seen sailors, or so-called, go down on their knees and pray. It was the fourth officer who told them it was no good asking Providence to save you if you did not try to save yourself and, without exaggeration, that fourth officer saved my life two or three times. After trying for 53 hours we managed to get the quadrant secure. It was a good job the storm abated somewhat, for we had to reeve off fresh steering chains round the outside of the poop, but we managed to do it only just in time, for we had driven well down into the Bay of Biscay.

Now, after the storm had fined down, the captain mustered all hands and gave them praise for the way we stuck to our duty; for he said that if he had had a coolie crew he was certain that he would have lost the ship.

37

You should have seen the state of the troop decks for, with nearly two thousand troops being battened down, they could not sling their hammocks up in the storm and laid about anywhere, and all, or nearly all, sea-sick. Now on going through the Straits of Gibraltar the ship must have looked as though she had had a washing day, for the *Victoria* was a four-masted vessel and, after the hurricane, the soldiers' bedding, etc, was in such a state with their sea-sickness that one of us sailors was put over 50 of them to get all their bedding and hammocks on deck. So the 50 soldiers with deck brooms and the ship-water hose had to scrub all the bedding and hammocks. After they was drained off a bit, we hoisted them up line upon line from the truck, or top of the mast, stretching them from mast to mast right down to the deck, and that is how the ship was dressed with drying clothes going through the Straits of Gibraltar.

Anyhow we arrived at Malta all safe. Then the diver went down and examined the stern post and rudder and the steam and hand steering gear was properly repaired. Then we proceeded on our way for Bombay. We coaled ship at Port Said, then proceeded through the Suez Canal. Then, even in fine weather, we found out the Cockney sailors, for going through the Canal there were 12, one after the other, turned away from the steering wheel till it was my turn. I went to the wheel and the fourth officer said, 'I think this chap will do.' So receiving orders from the pilot, with the captain and officers standing round, I steered as directed for perhaps a quarter-of-an-hour when the pilot said to the captain, 'This man will do.' So the captain said I was to go on steering till we was through the Canal. I was at the wheel ten hours, then the captain said I was to have a day off and after that be a day hand ready for any other emergency.

We reached Bombay and discharged our troops, reloaded with homeward-bound troops and reached England, back at

Southampton, after a very pleasant and fine run. We landed our troops at Portsmouth, then proceeded to Southampton to clean up and make all ready for the next trip. It was while we were in Southampton Docks that the skipper of the yacht *Ellen* asked me if I would go with him as mate of the *Ellen* to Germany again. So I told him I would if I could get clear of the troopers. So going on board the next morning, I went to the captain and asked him for my discharge, but he would not hear of it. He said now he had got a good sailor, he was going to try and keep him. As I was leaving his cabin I saluted, but in this salute I gave a sign of an Order I belonged to and left the cabin. But I had only got about a dozen steps away when the captain's servant called me back as the captain wanted to speak to me. And then it proved that him and myself belonged to the same Order. Then he said that he would try and get the company to sanction my discharge, as of course I had signed on for the trooping season and we had only made one voyage, whereas three voyages was the amount of trips made in the trooping season. As I was determined to leave, he said he was very sorry to lose me, as he said he was discharging one of the boatswain's mates and was going to rate me for the position; but I explained to him that yachting was my ambition in life, so eventually he secured my discharge, and I left much to the regret of all the officers, especially the fourth officer. I went to his cabin to get a pass out for my kit and we had a parting drink and wished each other God speed and good luck. But I am, or was, sorry that I left, as it turned out, for after the *Victoria* had left on her next voyage the captain of the yacht *Ellen* where I was to go mate, came and told me he was sorry he could not take me, as he had had news from his owner to say he had to have a German mate. That was hard luck on me after giving up a ship where I might have got on in the company, which I found out when I met the captain of the troopship

39

later. Well, anyhow, things like this do happen to some and I happened to be one of them left out of work. I stopped out of work till Christmas 1894.

* * *

In 1894 I decided I would stay at home and try working in Southampton Docks. I worked for the shore boatswain and also for Livetts and Franks, sailor painter, painting any ship they had a contract for. They generally painted the East Indian Company. The skipper of one ship would only have sailor painters on board to do the cabin as well as the outside, for he reckoned the sailor painter was better than the painter of that trade.

Well, I continued at that during the 1894–1895 winter. Then for the '95 summer season the Earl of Dunraven had a cruising yacht of 90 tons named L'Esperance[2] so I went to her in March, 1895 and helped fit her out till they were ready to fit out the Earl's new 20-rater, Audrey[3], at Payne's Yacht Yard at Southampton. Then I shipped on her as AB under Captain Bevis. After she was ready for sailing, we raced her at Harwich and from there to Southend Pier against five other yachts of the same class, winning several first prizes. One of our rivals was a Yankee 20-rater, Niagara[4], come over from America, and when we had finished racing up the east coast, we had beaten the American five times and she had beaten us four times. Then, when we all got to Southampton, our class parted, half going to the Clyde for the summer races and us who was named Audrey remaining inside the Isle of Wight where they had fixed as many regattas as there were on the Clyde. Anyhow, we managed at the end of the season to have 16 first prizes and 12 others out of 32 starts – not bad, with about 12 yachts entering in most races. We had a good pay day when we finished. We fitted out the skipper's fishing boat, raced her at Bursledon

Regatta and won the first prize, ending up with an enjoyable day, all yachtsmen and fishermen joining together in making all the fun.

We paid off from the *Audrey* with a promise from the captain that we could come back to her the next season when it was time to fit out for the 1896 season. Then I shipped in the Union Castle ship *Scot* making two voyages to the Cape of Good Hope in the winter.

6
Under the Kaiser

a vow that if ever I had / I made / charge of a Ship I would never / take the landlords of a pub / out for a sail for allthough, / we had them on board all / that we had to drink till then / was two glasses of lager Beer

In 1896, in March, I shipped with Captain Miles in the American-built 20-rater Isolde[1] as AB. She was laid up in Germany at Krupp's Yard at Kiel. We went over as passengers in a North German Mail ship to Hamburg, going from there to Kiel by train. We fitted her out at Krupp's Yard and raced in all the Baltic regattas till it was time to come to England for the racing in the Solent.

It was while we was at Kiel that I had two accidents. First, the skipper decided to go out for a trial sail so that we should pull everything in place and get everything ship-shape for the race and, as luck would have it, the captain took some friends along for pleasure; they were landlords of hotels. We sailed around Kiel Bay and landed one of them at the entrance of the Kiel Canal, myself and another AB putting him ashore in the dinghy and picking up another friend there, he bringing a gallon cask of beer with him. We got it on board the dinghy, placing the cask under the seat. But the German! What a size he was! He said he weighed 22 stone and he was bigger round than the barrel of beer. The yacht was sailing about in the meantime waiting for us. Now we had to be careful, we sailors in the dinghy, for she was a very cranky boat and it was a dangerous job with a big German on board, and he not used to a boat and the yacht sailing about, manoeuvring to pick us up. So I being the after-man rowing, took both the paddles while the bow-man had the boat's tow-line ready to throw to the yacht when she shot up head to wind to pick us up. I had warned the German to sit perfectly still and not move whatever happened. So I said, 'Stand by with the rope, Dan!'; and 'Sit still,' to the German.

At this moment the yacht came up head to wind, but before the bow-man could throw the line the big German jumped upright putting both hands on the side of the boat and turned her over, putting the three of us in the water. Now I myself could not swim a stroke. I having both paddles, thrust myself clear of the boat and lost one of the paddles, but clung on to the other. I noticed the German clinging to the overturned boat. I thought I should have been all right, but I heard my mate come blowing up behind me. He could only swim a little and he caught hold of the paddle what was keeping me afloat. Well, it was not buoyant enough to support two, so we sank. I lost the paddle and my mate had it. As the yacht passed us I saw Jack Jewett jump overboard. I knew what he was going to do, for he knew I could not swim. When I saw him jump overboard that was the last I knew, for I felt I was going down for the last time. I did not remember a thing after that till I came to my senses. They were rolling me about on the deck of the yacht and using artificial respiration. I was throwing up salt water, so that is how I know what it is to be drowned.

As Jack Jewett told me after that, he let me go down the third time, then he could have a better chance of saving me, as I should not struggle. He was the strongest swimmer I had known in my life. I had been shipmates with him in a good many ships and we were always good chums, especially after that. It was after that turn that I made a vow that if ever I had charge of a ship I would never take the landlord of a pub out for a sail, for although we had them on board, all that we had to drink till then was two glasses of lager beer. The captain was a bit frightened, for he said we must keep quiet about it, as what would people say having four or five landlords of pubs on board. We were invited ashore that evening, and I will admit that I could have had too much to drink, but I would only take it in moderation. They must have spoken about it, for when I passed any German that evening they started the motion of swimming; but it soon wore off.

Now the other accident I mentioned was after that, when we was racing. I was masthead man. I was at the masthead. It was raining and I had to do something in a hurry, and everything was wet. I was sending down the topsail, when I slipped, falling but bringing myself up with my hands. This caused a sudden jerk and a pain in my groin. I called out to Jack Jewett to come up to me. Being a strong chap I reckoned he saved my life again, or at least a very bad accident. I had to go on shore to a doctor. He wanted me to go in a German hospital and let them operate as I had been ruptured. But I would not and wore the belt that probably saved my life again later.

We left Germany shortly after and got to Southampton in time to clean up for the regattas inside the Isle of Wight. It was then I had a week's sick leave and it was while I was home when the accident to Isolde occurred and the owner, Baron von Zedwitz, was killed; he died when they were rushing him ashore and this is how it was told to me while I was home resting.

Two of the crew's wives came to my home and told me there had been a terrible accident to the Isolde. Had I heard about it? I said 'No.' You remember there are two Isolde's, one 40 tons and one 20 tons. That's how they were rated. On 18th August 1896 they were racing at Southsea. I got on the 'phone to Nicholson's Yard and they told me it was the Isolde the 20-ton German yacht. The largest class and the 20-tonners met at the starting boat of the first round. They was all of a heap, the larger ones overtaking the smaller; as the Isolde was rounding the mark, the Satanita struck the Isolde a glancing blow. The Emperor of Germany's yacht Meteor[2], following close behind, ran straight into the Isolde, striking her right over the cockpit where the owner was sitting. The wire bobstay cut through the Isolde's side to the water's edge and cut right across the owner's chest and knocked the mast, sails and everything down. The chap that had taken my place jumped overboard and was saved by a naval pinnace. The owner was found under the mainsail still alive, but he died while the naval launch was taking him to Ryde, Isle of Wight. It was a lucky business there was no more of the crew injured. That finished the Isolde's career and now this is where the Earl of Dunraven came in.

Hearing that all the Isolde's crew was being paid off, he sent Captain Bevis of his 20-tonner Audrey to say if the crew of the Isolde would care to fit the Audrey out in a hurry, we could finish the racing season in her. So we accepted the job, fitted her out, and was in time to race her at Weymouth, Torquay, Dartmouth and going as far down as Plymouth. Luck and handling her was the means of us winning two first prizes at each place[3]. He said we had given him a good sporting time. He paid us for 12 first prizes in the place of eight wins; very good of him. We took the Audrey back to Southampton, and laid her up for the winter; so we done very well, paid off from Isolde with £18 prize money and £12 from Audrey, making £30 in all. Very good in all, what?

* * *

After we laid the Audrey up, I decided to have another winter on shore and work about the Southampton Docks till the time came

The German Emperor's *Meteor*. © Beken of Cowes.

in 1897 to look for a yacht. Oh, by the way, after the accident to *Isolde*, the *Meteor* was taken to Scotland and laid up for the winter on the Clyde, and Captain Gomes, the captain of her at the time of the accident with *Isolde*, was paid off, and in January, 1897, my cousin Captain Ben Parker was put in charge. In March of that year I had a letter from him asking me if I would go as AB in her,

if so, I could join her as soon as he got to the River Itchen. He
was sailing for there the latter part of March. The *Meteor* arrived at
Itchen on the 1st April. I went direct on board and was fixed up
as AB for as long as I liked to stay, or as long as Captain Parker had
charge of her. He was fixed for ten years with her. The Emperor
of Germany was the owner. So we carried on and fitted her out,
racing at Harwich and going in all the races around the English
coast, and at Bangor in Ireland, before going over to Kiel for the
racing there, Eckernforde and Travemünde and then returning to
England for the racing at Cowes, Ryde, Southsea, Southampton
and Weymouth. While I was bow-man of the Emperor's gig I
found that the Kaiser was a real sportsman and very gentlemanly.
While on board we got 24 prizes.

There is one thing I must write about which ought to have
been in the order of writing, as I came along. We arrived at Kiel
three days before the Kiel Regattas started, and we had on board
a German admiral to represent the Kaiser, while the Kaiser should
be absent. We also had aboard Lord Lonsdale, who was a great
friend of the Kaiser. The Emperor was out on his steam yacht in
the Baltic watching the German Fleet manoeuvres. We, the crew
of the Kaiser's gig, had to be ready to take Admiral Eisendecker
on board the Kaiser's steam yacht, and it was our job to try to be
quickest on board, so that the admiral would be the first to greet
the Kaiser as soon as the fleet of the German Navy arrived and
moored up to their stations. Admiral Eisendecker said to us that it
would be a great honour for him, and us, to be first on board, but
we had to watch for a signal to start; that meant we should have
to race against about a dozen gigs and whalers, one each from
the other vessels.

Anyhow, as soon as the signal went, we started. We had about
three-quarters of a mile to go and, boys, what a row! But we was
first on board, but only just, with the Kaiser watching from the

Tom's cousin, Captain Ben Parker, wearing the workaday uniform
of a yacht crew.

bridge of his yacht. The Kaiser was greatly pleased, for when he
came on board of the *Meteor* he asked us, the gig's crew, to go and
stand before him. As we stood there he thanked us for being such
oarsmen and complimented us on the handling of his gig and
expressed his wish that we would be his regular gig crew, and,
when he went back to his steam yacht, we rowed him to it; he

said when we left him there that we was a smart crew. We also thought at the time that it was a great honour. Let me mention that the Meteor had a crew of 44 all-told, 42 English and two Germans, who were mostly used for interpreters, as they could speak English having sailed in English and American sailing ships.

We laid the Meteor up at White's yacht yard. Twelve ABs was to stay and work by her all the winter. They had to include the gig's crew and I was one of them. You can always find plenty to do in a large racing yacht of the Meteor's size. So we 12 worked at her rigging, renewing almost everything – for there is tremendous heavy strain and wear and tear in a yacht of this kind. A racing captain is a wise man if he renews everything of his rigging. He is more sure, then, of himself and can dare things more than otherwise – than if he had not renewed his gear. But there are sometimes owners who cannot or will not stand the price of renewal. It is on this sort of yacht that there are the most accidents. So we carried on and we were told we must not have an accident with the German Emperor on board.

The 1st of March, 1897, we shipped the remainder of the crew to make the full crew of 44 all told, and we was made to understand that we was to carry half Germans and half English as able seamen. So, of course, we English used to yarn and talk about it amongst ourselves, and say, now we are going to learn the Germans. Very soon we commented they would be all Germans on his yacht and you could see how the Kaiser was increasing his naval fleet. So we carried on the same as in 1896, going in all the same races, but when we started the races we found the English clubs had put double our handicap time allowance on us. The Meteor was the largest craft in our class, and the time allowed on the yacht Caress, a 60-rater, in 1896 by the Meteor was 14½ minutes on a 35-mile course. Now in 1897 the time was altered for the 35-mile course. The *Meteor* had allowed the 60-ton yacht 29 minutes. Anyone with any common sense could have seen that with a fair sailing breeze all the class going round the course would do it so quick there would not be time enough for the largest yacht to save her time. We pointed it out to the Kaiser, but he said he was a sportsman and it was the rule laid down[4]. It was not right, but he would race all the same. So as a result we only had 12 prizes instead of like the year before (1896) 24.

There is one incident that happened to me in this year. That was while we was racing at Travemünde in the Baltic. There was a very hard wind blowing and a nasty sea. We was getting plenty of water over up. While we was putting the ship on to the other tack something knocked me on the head, taking the skin and hair off the top of it and I was blinded with the blood and salt water. They got me below. The Kaiser saw it and sent his doctor to me. He bandaged me up when we got in port. The Kaiser came to me and said I could go to the best hospital in Germany, but I told him it was not bad enough. Anyhow, he shook hands with me and hoped I would be all right for Cowes week in England. I thought that was very humble of him. That was the last race in Germany, and when he came to Cowes I was on deck and, after greeting the admiral and officers, he came and enquired of my welfare and shook my hand again, saying he was glad I was looking so well.

So we carried on racing till the end of the racing season only getting 12 prizes in 1897. The Kaiser left us and we took the *Meteor* to White's Yard again, laid her up for the winter and paid all off except us same 12, who were kept on for the winter to do as we had done the winter before. So there we were overhauling and replacing new rigging. It was in February, 1898, I was renewing the wire jib halyards when our captain called and said he wanted to speak to me, and the first words he said to me was, 'Do you know that you are not going to race in the Meteor this coming season of 1898, or I hardly think so.'

I replied, 'What's the reason? Have I done anything wrong?' He answered, 'I do not think so, but keep this quiet under your hat. I will let you know more later.' So of course that kept me wondering. I kept that way, wondering, till the middle of March, then the captain, seeing me by myself, asked me to call at his home at 6.30pm that evening.

So of course I called at his home at the time appointed. The captain said, 'I want a quiet chat with you. I am sorry to disappoint you, but it is up to you now after you have heard what I tell you whether you stop in the Meteor this year or not. You remember I told you some time ago that I did not think that you would be sailing in the Meteor this year. Well, I had a letter from a high official in Germany to the effect that they had been keeping an eye on you since you had been on board the Meteor and they thought you was a likely chap for a job in another yacht they had in mind for you, Tom, providing the captain's report of you was good.'[5]

So the captain said he wrote back and said I could fill the job as well as he, the captain, could himself, as I had been taught under the same teacher as himself and, though young, I had had the experience of racing in racers of all classes in England. And now comes the final test. When this high official wrote to the captain again he said when he had an answer from the owner of the yacht he had already got a man for skipper, but he asked whether I would take the place of mate for the summer or whether I would take the place as skipper if they took the man away. I answered at once I would take the mate's job. The captain said he was glad I took it and said, 'That way, Tom, they will think more of you still. I will tell you now it is the highest official in Germany'; and he said they would be keeping their eye on me in the new job. The captain said he did not have to tell me that, but he said it just to warn me. I could keep on working in Meteor till the 15th of April, 1898, when I was to take on the mate's job of the 15-metre cutter Marolga[6]. We was to have eight in the crew, the captain, myself as mate, one German AB and five English ABs. So of course I left for Germany on the 15th of April for Hamburg.

* * *

The yacht Marolga had been built at Max Oertz's yard, opposite to Hamburg, named Neuhoff am Reiherstieg. We found her already built, so we set to and rigged her out and sailed her down the River Elbe and through the Kiel Canal. We had to row through that; then sailed down the Baltic for 90 miles to Travemünde, the port where the two owners lived. Two owners, mind you, we did not bargain for that. It would have been all right if they had both been on board together. But as soon as one had finished sailing and we stowed up for the night the other would come and say to the captain, 'We will sail around Travemünde Bay till 12 o'clock because my frau wants to see the moon rise up out of the water.' It used to be 1.30 or 2am in the morning by the time we turned in then. After a day like that the skipper would say, 'Call me at a quarter to six, Tom, so that I can tell what the weather will be like for the day.'

I said, 'Why do you want it that way, skipper? Why not take the day as it comes? As a matter of fact, do you know it's started a new day and no one has had any rest?'

'Well,' he said, 'Turn in, I will tell you in the morning when you turn out.'

So being all tired out we turned in our bunks. Anyhow I woke up at 6am called all hands and the skipper said, 'There is no time to scrub the decks. The other owner wants to sail at 6.30am to be back by 10 o'clock for business.' I said, 'Why did you not tell me last night, I might have altered that.' He answered, 'You are here to do as you are told!' All I answered was, 'Quite so!'

We laid right close to the house of the owner what was going for a sail this morning. He came on board at 6.45am, had a sail out in the Bay of Travemünde, returning to the harbour at 9.45am. So I accosted the gentleman before he went on shore and asked him if the other owner and himself would come on board together in the evening as myself and the crew would like to have a talk with them. He said he would see the other gentleman and I could take his word that he would be there. He went at that, so the skipper asked me what I had asked him that for. I told him he could be there to listen if he liked. 'Ask yourself,' says I, 'how many times have I asked you to do what I am going to do!'

So the evening came with the owners, and they said, 'Well what is it Mr Diaper?'

My answer, 'Well, sirs, as spokesman for myself and the crew, I would like to mention we have not started racing yet. I would like to know if you are going racing?'

'Yes,' they answered.

'Well then, sirs, do you know that sailing night time with a heavy dew falling with all new sails up, you are spoiling them? If you continue to do so you will spoil them for racing.'

They turned to the captain and asked him whether that was so.

He said, 'Everyone says so, sir.'

'Well,' they answered, 'why did you not tell us so? Now no more night sailing before we start racing.'

So after that we went out daytime in fine weather. Well, taking the racing through that season we did not do very well, but when we raced at Copenhagen we won the first two days and the third day a Danish boat took the first prize. We busted our bows in. The wind blew very hard so we returned to Hamburg, and laid the *Marolga* up in her winter quarters at Oertz's. On the morning that I and the crew was to catch the steam boat for home, the designer asked the German AB to tell me Mr Oertz wanted me. I saw him. He told me he had an order to build a new 12-metre for a Berlin gentleman. Would I come back to Germany at any time he would send for me? I replied that I would. With that he pressed a 100-mark note in my hand and wished me God speed.

The German AB chap could speak English, having been in English sailing ships. He had told me during the summer that some of his countrymen was watching me very closely and he thought I should hear something to my advantage, and when I saw the captain of the Meteor he said that he heard that I had made good.

* * *

Arriving in England after a hard summer's racing I found that I was in great pain with my hernia, what I contracted in the Isolde two years before, so my dear wife persuaded me to go to my doctor and so I did. He examined me and said the best thing I could do for my own good was to go in hospital and be operated on. So after waiting three weeks for a bed to be ready for me, I went in the Royal South Hants and Southampton Hospital. They operated and it was a success, for I have not found anything the matter with that side since. I was all well when I came out of hospital, three weeks before Christmas, 1898. I was quite OK by Christmas and we had an enjoyable one. In the evening of Christmas day I received a telegram from Max Oertz of Hamburg, Germany, asking me if it was all right for me to come over to Hamburg at once, as he wanted me as soon as I could get there. So I wired back to say I would catch the boat train from Victoria and cross to Flushing the next night, arriving in Hamburg on the 28th December, 1898. So I did, and I arrived at Max Oertz's yard mid-day on the 28th December and found that Oertz, the designer, had left for Berlin and I should follow on as soon as I could. So the foreman of the yacht yard took me to the large boat-shed, and on my enquiring what was that they were building, his answer was it was a 12-metre racer, *Klein Polly*[7]. She was for a Berlin gentleman and I was to go on to Berlin at once. I had a quick lunch with the foreman and he took me to the Hamburg Bahnhof railway station and wired Berlin I was on the way, and when the train got to Friedrichstrasse Bahnhof, Max Oertz was there to receive me. He had a cab and he took me to Prince's Hotel where I had dinner. He thought I would like an English beefsteak and he was about right, for I was hungry. After dinner he explained all about the job and was glad I had acted so promptly, as the owner was rather an abrupt man and wanted to see me at 10 o'clock sharp the next morning.

I turned in to get a good night, for I could never sleep in a train, so next morning Oertz took me to the barber's where I had a good shave and smarten up and got to the office of Mr Buxenstein, 240/241 Friedrichstrasse, the main business street of Berlin. There I met the good gentleman. He was a man on the big side, 6 feet 3 inches and big built, and he made me look rather small and he seemed to me of a rather forceful type.

'Ah, well,' I thought, 'I am an Englishman and act as such, we being the leading yachtsmen and the Germans only have us to learn them how to make their sailors smart.'

As I had found out the German sailor man was a good seaman, but they all seemed to be very awkward about the feet. So as I was introduced, I was glad I had been shipmates with Germans.

So he asked if I was prepared to take skipper of this yacht. I told him I was certainly able to do so. After that we had a talk and, both from his side and from my own side, we came to a proper understanding and agreed with one another. His first words were, 'Have you had charge of a racer before.'

I truthfully answered that I had been in charge of the Earl of Dunraven's 5-ton yacht *Alwida* and mate of Count Douglas' yacht with a German crew, and mate of the *Marolga*, a German yacht also. He agreed to all that I said. Then he surprised me by saying that I had been recommended to him by the first man and highest in Germany. He himself was the German Kaiser's right hand to arrange the Kaiser's sports besides being the biggest newspaper man in Germany. Well we came to agree on wages, racing money, food money for the five English including the mate in the crew. When it come to the two German AB sailors I was to carry, he said that the Germans' pay was to be through the Kaiserlichen Yacht Club. The wages per week was 18 marks and racing money was ten marks first prize, five marks second prize, and nothing for a third or losing.

'Well,' he says, 'that is all I am allowed to pay them.'

'Well, sir,' I replied, 'I am sorry but I will not take the job under those conditions.'

'That should be all right,' he says.

I replied, 'It might be for you but it can't do for me. The English able seamen get two pound wages per week, one pound ten shillings first prize, one pound second prize, ten shillings third, ten shillings losing money, and three shillings a day food money. On racing days for English and German sailors working together doing the same work, what would be the result? It would not be right. I will take the job of skipper willingly if you will pay them the same as the *Meteor* is paying.'

Eventually he agreed providing it was not known outside the crew that they was getting more than Germany's wages for sailors. So everything was settled and I had to be in Hamburg to superintend the finishing of building of the yacht *Polly*[8], on the

1st of March, 1899, the rest of the crew starting the 1st day of May. Anyway, we started racing at Hamburg, then Brunsbuttel at the Elbe end of the Kiel canal, then Cuxhaven 18 miles below the canal on the Elbe, then at Kiel. By this time the owner was pleased and had given an order to Max Oertz to design and build a two-rater for the fall races on the inland lakes of Berlin. So after we had been to Travemünde, Swinemünde, Warnemünde, Memel, Riga and Sandham at the entrance to Stockholm we had raced two times in all and got 20 first prizes. We returned from Stockholm to Hamburg and laid the Polly up for the winter. We still had the two-rater Klein Polly (meaning Small Polly). We paid the crew off and sent them home and kept back my brother Jack who was mate, and Jack Hulberg (one of the Germans and a nice German too) and myself, taking the Klein Polly inside a barge up the canal to Berlin. There under a crane we lifted the Klein Polly out of the barge and towed her to the Wannsee Lake where we raced six times and got six first prizes. Then we unstepped the mast and towed her on the canal through the heart of Berlin close to the Reichstag, the German House of Parliament, and on through to the Müggelsee Lake where we made ready and raced six more races there. We gained six more first prizes, making 13 prizes in all, for they gave a prize for the boat that took most prizes. So the owner was very pleased with the way I had managed and handled the two yachts and we had had a very good summer. Nothing went wrong. He thanked me much as also did Mrs Buxenstein and said they both hoped to see me the following season of 1900. So, wishing me good luck and God speed, we parted and we laid the Klein Polly up at a yard on the Müggelsee Lake. We paid off, took the train to Hamburg, and took the boat to Harwich, train to London and Southampton Docks Station, and then a cab from there to the good old village of Itchen, our home where we found all the family.

I forgot to mention that before I had left Berlin, Mr Buxenstein had said that I might be wanted over to Berlin somewhere about the middle of January, 1900, as the German Emperor had asked him if he would be able to send *Klein Polly* to represent Germany in some races with boats of other countries. So I said I would be ready when ever he sent for me. I gave a guess that it would be the South of France, but we shall see for sure later.

So ends the year 1899 having done very well.

7
Racing *Klein Polly*

*That was where I done well
Winning Every day first Prizes
I the Poll. after finishing in Polly
I would Sail in Klein Polly. I
Can Safelly Say I Won 5 prizes on
day at Keel 3 in Polly Beating
the Kaisers "Meteor" on Time on all
Courses and Klein Polly beating them
all the Same Way as Polly*

Now we come to the year 1900. It was the 7th of January, 1900, when I received a letter from Mr Buxenstein asking me to be in Berlin the 15th January, bringing my mate with me and leaving him in Hamburg in lodgings, while I went on to Berlin to get my instructions regarding what I was to do with the *Klein Polly*. So me and my mate travelled to Germany, via the London-Harwich to Hamburg route. Leaving the mate at Hamburg, I went on to Berlin and when I went to the boss's office he told me to go to the Müggelsee where the *Klein Polly* was laid up. He had already given the order to have the boat sent to Hamburg by the time I got there, to see if everything was in apple-pie order. When I arrived at Müggelsee Yard and inspected I found the boat was already on the train, all her gear as well. Everything was correct, and ready to leave for Max Oertz's Yacht Werft, Hamburg; so I returned to the office, got my instructions and everything to take the *Klein Polly* to the South of France.

I arrived at Hamburg before the boat, connected with my mate and the German chap Jack Hulberg. I had wired for him to meet me at Oertz's Yacht Werft from his home on Rugen Island in the Baltic, hoping the boat would arrive at the yard before the steam boat arrived what was to take her on board. The *Klein Polly* arrived at the yard the next day, so two days after the steamer arrived we was going to float her across the river Elbe to the steamer. But in the meantime it froze so hard that the river had frozen over. The ice was 3 inches thick and so much traffic had broken it up, and the tide running 6 miles an hour had so many ice floes that we decided to hire eight horses and a strong lorry to take the yacht round by road. We had to muffle the wheels with ropes and chains, the roads were so icy. We got her on board, lifting her by the heavy crane and got her properly secured. This steam boat was taking her as far as Havre. Then we was to put her on board a French Translantic ship to take her from Havre as far as Marseilles. We found on arriving at Havre that the other ship would not get there for another five days and the German steamship could not stay that long. So the crane took us off her deck and put us in the Dock Harbour. This being a case of waiting five days, and being on a Thursday, I left her in the dock-master's and the mate's hands and caught the night mailboat to Southampton, arriving home on Friday morning. My wife was surprised as she thought I was on the way to Marseilles. Anyhow I had two nights home, besides seeing Southampton beating Newcastle by one goal to nil at the Dell in the Cup.

I returned to Havre on Sunday night. The French steamer arrived on Tuesday morning. We put our boat on board and secured her properly by 12 noon and was told we ought to be on board by 7pm for dinner.

Now I can say in the German boat from Hamburg we lived like lords, with four good meals a day and coffee first thing in the morning. But in the French boat we only had two meals a day and no coffee in the morning. Breakfast at 10am was a bottle of red wine and a loaf of bread, nothing else. For dinner we had a plate of soup as one course, about one ounce of meat for second course, and we had to eat that first before the third course, which consisted of a spoonful of cabbage. The fourth course was a potato – one, mind you, cut in halves; but we had a first-class cabin. I saw the captain and offered to pay five francs a day for each of us for extra food, but he said he would have done it, only he was frightened of the other captain. He told me the ship was a reserve ship and was double-manned with officers, from the captain down to the junior officer. I can tell you we was pleased when we got to the South of France.

When we were entering the port of Marseilles just at dark we saw a man in a row boat. We called him and we put a rope over the side and slid down it into the boat. He put us ashore and we found a cafe where we had a good feed of ham and eggs and coffee; and what a fill-out, for we were nearly starved! But I knew we should not have left the ship like that. We ought to have waited till the captain had cleared the ship and the port doctor had cleared her. We slept on shore that night, and, my! when we appeared on board there was trouble. Our German Secretary was on board and he spoke French. He told me they was going to put us in gaol, but I explained all about it and told him I would never sail in a French ship again and he would have to put the Klein Polly on a German ship or an English one, for she was too small to sail back to Germany. Anyway the doctor run the rule over us and cleared us and they let us go free.

Well we got Klein Polly off the deck into the water and a small boat towed us round to the yacht harbour, where we moored her stern on to the quay. We went and engaged lodgings at the Sailors' Home for the three of us. So after a night's rest we went down to the harbour and rigged *Klein Polly* and made her ready for racing. We had three days' racing at Marseilles, taking all three first prizes. Then we left for Cannes, raced there, then at Nice and Monte Carlo. We started in 22 races. We broke our main boom one day at Cannes and on another day at Cannes we carried away our mast. Of course we had to be towed to the harbour.

Now the boss said we had a spare mast and asked where it was. I said it was at Nice as I could not get a conveyance at Marseilles to drop it at Cannes. Nice, 20 miles further east was the nearest place where I could get it sent. I said we would have to hire horses and a lorry to bring it from Nice by road to the dock. So he said, 'Being as I can speak French I will go with you, in the train. We race again tomorrow. Do you hope to be ready?'

I said, 'Yes, I want to surprise the boats in our class.'

So we took the train at 4pm, got to Nice and saw the broker who had charge of the spars, two sets in two 45-feet-long cases. We hired six horses and a lorry, saw the cases put on the lorry, then the boss called the lorry man to him. The boss took out of his pocket a gold 20 franc piece. Showing it to the driver he said, 'The captain will give you this if you are at the beach end of the Cannes harbour by five minutes to 12 midnight.' It was 7.30pm when all was ready to start. The boss gave me the gold piece and we left by train and returned to Cannes.

There were several yachts from my home village of Itchen. Their crews offered to help, so we went to the beach end at 11.45pm and the lorry arrived at 11.52pm, eight minutes before the appointed hour of midnight. So I gave the driver the gold 20 francs; and pleased? I should say he was!

We unloaded the lorry and all promised to be at that spot at 4 o'clock in the morning. We surprised our class when they saw us sailing around pulling everything in place. The Frenchmen knew that I had ordered a new mast to be made, and as they knew it could not be made in time for the race that day, of course they wanted to know how we secured a new mast.

We raced that day and won the first prize. Altogether we got 19 prizes out of 21 starts and only lost on the two days we had the accidents.

On the last day we wired to Marseilles for the largest and fastest tow-boat to come and tow us from Cannes to Marseilles as fast as he could. He arrived next morning at 4am and we was all ready for him. We had two tow-lines of 100 fathoms each. After about four hours' towing it came on to blow a gale of wind and rain. We could not see the tow-boat and he could not see us. We was in that for four hours. All that I was afeared of was when we was running down to the hollow of a sea; for the waves was that big that I feared the tow-line would get around our keel and turn us over. The tow-lines wanted watching, the tow-lines was in a big loop each side of us. Well, at the end of four hours we rounded a headland. The water was smooth in a small bay, it was a bit sheltered and the tow-boat anchored and the skipper he pulled us alongside of him to know if we was still on the end of the tow-rope. The only thing he could do during the storm was to go as fast as he could make for the small bay he knew of.

'And glad I am to get here,' says he.

I wired to Marseilles and told the secretary. The place was called Aga Bay. We stayed there that day, the weather abated in the night and we left early next morning, arriving 6 o'clock in the evening, the same time as the German steamer that was to take her to Hamburg in Germany. We got the *Klein Polly* hoisted on deck, made her secure for to leave first thing in the morning. My brother was the mate and the German AB was to go with the boat. They was glad it was a German ship for they knew they would have plenty of food, not starved like on the French ship coming out. I stood by till she left; then I caught the train to Paris and Havre, thence to

Southampton by boat. I was to have ten days' holiday, then to take the rest of the crew for the big Polly for the racing in Germany. I shipped the four same men that I had come to Southampton to ship for the Polly in 1899, so that was good for me. As soon as my holiday expired I took the four men and went to Germany via Southampton, London and Harwich to Hamburg. I found the Klein Polly had arrived two days ahead of me, so that was all right. We fitted out both the Polly and Klein Polly, as the owner wanted both at the Kiel Regatta week.

That was where I done well, winning every day first prizes in the Polly. After finishing in Polly I would sail in Klein Polly. I can safely say I won five prizes one day at Kiel, three in Polly beating the Kaiser's Meteor on time on all courses, and again in Klein Polly beating them all the same way as Polly. We did not go to Denmark, Sweden or Norway; but any way, we was the top of the Polly class and Klein Polly also. The owner said we wanted a spell, so I think the following copy of the testimony will finish 1900 well.

Copy of Testimony, Berlin, 21st December, 1900.

Mr Thomas Diaper of Itchen Ferry has acted during the two summers of 1899 and 1900 as master of the German racing yacht, 'Polly,' 30 tons TM, also during the winter racing season 1899–1900 in the Mediterranean as master of the racing yacht 'Klein Polly,' both yachts owned by me. I will testify very willingly that Mr Diaper fulfilled all his duties as a racing skipper and master of the crew in a very satisfactory way. He did his best to maintain discipline, cleanliness and general good conduct of the crew. He kept both yachts smart, tidy and clean, and yacht conditions and the drill of his crew was always admired at yachting stations in Germany, Denmark, Sweden and France. Mr Diaper himself was always willing to fulfil the owner's requests in a good manner and he has always acted very skilfully at the tiller lines when racing, both yachts always being at the top of the class. I wish him cheerfully a similar good success in his further career as master of a racing yacht.

Signed: Georg Buxenstein

That ends 1900.

8
An Emperor's Praise

The Emperor got on board. and said wonder Boat you say and now I want to see the other wonder Mr Stern what wonder do you mean your Magesty Why the man that handles the Boat Mr Stern Introduced Capt-Diaper your majesty.

Now in the year 1901 I had a letter from Mr Buxenstein to come over to Germany from the middle of May till the end of July, 1901, to fit out both the *Polly* and *Klein Polly* and race them the same as I had done in former years, and expressing the hope that I would have my usual success. I did, for we ended up the top of both classes again, and I received another good testimony of daring everything in the same skilful manner as before. Now before I left he told me the German Emperor had told him he would have to try an all-German crew, the skipper and all. He was sorry, for he had to obey. He would not be wanting me, or my crew, the next year; so that was that.

In the winter 1901–1902 I worked on board of several ships in Southampton Docks. The one I done most on was the troop ship *Canada*[1]. There was 12 of us put on her when she returned from taking troops to Cape Town. We done the sailors' work day-time, and stayed on board to act as firemen in case of a fire.

1902   I stayed in that job till the 1st of April. Then a large American steam yacht arrived on the River Itchen and I heard her owner was in want of a man who was used to racing in German waters. So I applied and got the job as skipper of their 8-metre racing yacht. I was to go to Hamburg and await her arrival there from New York. She was coming over the Atlantic on a steamer's deck. Well, she arrived in May with one American AB attached to her. So I shipped a German sailor to make our total of three to man her. We made her ready and sailed down the Elbe to Brunsbüttel, the entrance to the Kiel Canal. We towed through the Canal. When we got to Altenholz at the other end of the Canal, we slipped the tow and sailed to Bellevue where the Kaiser's Yacht Club Harbour was, and that was where we stayed, going out for a sail drill to get her tuned up for the racing season. While she was floating on the water she was the ugliest thing afloat, but if you saw her out of the water her design was the prettiest shape I had ever seen, but when floating the German sailors called her 'pigface,' and said she would be no good. All I said was, 'Wait and see.' Well, eventually Kiel Regatta started. The Head of the Club asked if he and me would have a bottle of sack, the same as he and me had together if Polly and Klein Polly won. We always drank one bottle to further success. Of course, I said, 'Yes.' He was a good friend, and umpire on my side if anything went wrong.

Well, the first day's regatta came and my old yacht was there with a German crew, and the same owner was there and he was on board. She started ten minutes before us. As I say, we started ten minutes behind her, and had to go the same course. We had only been sailing 30 minutes after our start (we was first boat in the 8-metre class) when we caught up to the Polly. The owner saw me and asked me if I would call and see him at the Kaiser's Yacht Club that night after the race. I said I would and called back as we passed, rather saucy, 'Goodbye, and I will see you if you are back in time.' I cannot tell you how far we beat the 12-metre class and our class, but we took three first prizes, first of our class, first for the fastest over the course and first for the area. I forgot to mention my yacht's name was *Virginia II*[2], and we had to sail to the Canal entrance to meet the owner as the steam yacht *Virginia*[3] was coming through. He had a surprise when he saw three winning flags and we had only raced once. I explained to him how it was. He said I had better be careful or the Germans in the other boats would be getting jealous. 'I know,' he said, 'as I am an American German.' (His wife was American, and a nice lady too). Both of them made a great fuss of me and I had to dine with them that night. After dinner I told him I had to go on shore and meet my late owner and have coffee with him at the Kaiser's Yacht Club. 'Very well,' he said, 'I have only been in Germany a few hours but I have heard you are very popular here,' and excused me. So I left to see my old owner, and what a welcome! The first words were, 'Well, Tom, tell me for God's sake how are you shipped in that ugly *Virginia* II? Not for good are you?' 'No, sir,' I replied.

Then he says, 'I want you back in *Polly* next year. You've got to come. I shall have a word to say to the Emperor for making me take German sailors. Look, I have not got a prize yet, and the German skipper is supposed to be the best man in Germany. Will you come back Tom?' 'Right, I am seeing the Emperor tonight. I will let you know tomorrow night for sure.'

So we raced all the races at Kiel, gaining seven first prizes in five races. Then on the Saturday we started at 8 o'clock in the morning in the ocean race from Kiel to Travemünde. We had to go inside Fehmarn Island, making 60 miles for us, while the other larger classes had to go around the island. We, as usual, got away with a good start, keeping the lead till we entered the channel between the island and the mainland. As is usually the case, if the leading boat does this, the others go a slightly different course. They might carry the wind all the way, and in this case that is what they did do. Anyway, we laid in a calm, not moving till just before dusk. All the others was away out of sight. When the breeze came to us, it was just as much as we wanted. 'Now lads,' I said, 'this is the way we like it best, the wind ahead. We will do our best, and see where we shall be at the finishing mark.' That was at 5.30pm and we had a 30-mile peg to windward, and I sailed that boat if ever a boat was sailed. We never saw any sail, or anything till we saw the searchlight flashing on the mark boat. We went past the finishing mark at two minutes to 1 o'clock. As we passed they fired a gun and cheered. The steam yacht *Virginia's* launch came and took us in tow for the harbour. Arriving there we moored alongside the steam yacht, and the owner had a good feed ready in the saloon for us. The German representative, a naval kapitan was there to represent the German clubs. A nice man he was! The owner told us not to worry about the morning, as he would go to the club and find out what we had done in the race. In the morning, about 10 o'clock we were busy doing odd jobs, when the owner came on board and said, 'Skipper, you can hoist up three prizes. First of your class. The first for doing the course the quickest, and the first for beating all classes.' So we had done well again. And then the German kapitan came on board and wanted the owner to go to the Club House to hear if the yarn what was going about was true.

So they went, and when they came back they said it was true. I asked what was it. It was that it was no use racing any more against the *Virginia II*, the boat and the men. 'So of course, Diaper,' the owner said to me, 'I am sorry, but I will not spoil the class, but they are racing tomorrow and could you take me out to watch

Racing in Germany in *Klein Polly*, Captain Tom Diaper at the helm.

the race and show me, by keeping out of their way, how you always manage to beat them, and they had left you so far behind yesterday.'

I said, 'Certainly.' So on top of that someone called out, 'The Emperor is coming, sir!' With that the owner went to receive the Emperor. The first words the Emperor said were, 'Mr Stern, can I look at your Wonder Boat?' The owner brought the Emperor round to the side where we was laying. He got on board and said, 'Wonder Boat you say; and now I want to see the other wonder.'

Mr Stern said, 'What wonder do you mean, your Majesty?'

'Why, the man that handles the boat.' Mr Stern then introduced Captain Diaper to His Majesty. The Emperor then turned, saw me and paused, looking hard. 'Why,' he said, putting out his hand which I took: 'Bow-man of my gig. So I am glad that it is only one man that has beaten me twice, instead of two different men with two yachts beating me twice.' Then he said, 'Your late owner of the Polly said he ordered you to stop Polly and let me in first, but the words you said to him was: "No sir. I am first and if I can manage it I am going to finish first. The Emperor is a sportsman. You ask him, sir, if I do the right thing by doing so in sport on the level." I told your owner you done right, Diaper. By the way, Stern, all your other class say they won't race against this man and boat any more, as they are too good. What are you going to do?'

'Well, your Majesty, I am telling Diaper he can sell her if he can find a buyer, or if not, in three months he is to pack her up and send her back to America.' The Emperor left then wishing me good luck and saying he may be seeing me next summer beating him again in the Polly.

Well, we went out the next day with the owner following our class around the course at a safe distance, not to interrupt them, but to show the owner how I handled her and how far I could have beaten them. So he said, when we got back, 'No wonder they won't race against you, but I am sorry it has cut your racing season short. Take her to Kiel, pay the two men off, you yourself sell her if you can at ten per cent commission, or pack her up and send her back to City Island, New York.'

So we left for Kiel and he left to go to Norway and cruise the Baltic.

So sailing out of the harbour we hoisted ten first prize flags, and the Germans was glad to see us go. I did not stay by the Virginia II the whole three months, but after six weeks I could not sell her, so I had permission to let the yard send her to America, while I went on board the Navahoe to pilot her in the race from Heligoland to Dover, and Dover to Ostend, at Ostend, and for the races inside the Isle of Wight.

So taking it on the whole, I had not done such a bad year. So when the Navahoe left Southampton I returned home well satisfied with what I had done in 1902.

The name of the German Representative: Naval Kapitan Begits of the School of Soundings for Torpedo Boats in the Baltic.

* * *

Now in the year of 1903 I went over to Hamburg 1st of May to rejoin the Polly with the same crew that I had in her before. When we had fitted her out for the Baltic races, we also fitted out the Klein Polly for the Kiel week.

We raced on the Elbe at Hamburg, Brunsbüttel and Cuxhaven, winning first prizes at all three places. We then returned to Hamburg and, taking Klein Polly with us, towed through the Kiel canal to Kiel for the Kiel week. We raced every day in the Polly, winning all six first prizes, and one day finished just in front of the Emperor's Meteor, taking the extra prize from her, making seven first prizes for the Polly, and transferring to Klein Polly, after Polly's races, to race Klein Polly, winning on all four days, making for me in the one week 11 wins at Kiel.

After that we went with Polly to Travemünde, Warnemünde, Swinemünde, Pillau, Memel, Copenhagen, Stockholm and Gothenburg, racing at all these places to the number of 22 races. We finished up by taking all the first prizes and three extra prizes, making for Polly 25 first prizes, and four wins for me in Klein Polly, making a total of 29 in all on the Baltic. The owner told me he was very pleased with me, wanting to know why I could win in Polly, whereas the Germans did not win one prize in the summer when he had to have them instead of the English. He said he could see the difference.

Well, we returned to Hamburg and laid the *Polly* up at Oertz's Werft and paid off the crew and sent them home, all but my brother and one German. I took them with me, and the *Klein Polly*, to Berlin for the fall races on the inland lakes.

We raced four races on the Lake Wannsee, five on the Müggelsee and took the three extra prizes for doing the fastest over the course of all classes what was racing.

Now before I finish with 1903 this is what the Empress of Germany said to the English steward, to tell me if he should see me. The Empress had, with interest, watched the *Polly's* doings from her schooner *Iduna*[4]. She was talking with the Emperor about the smart *Polly* and her winnings, and asked whether he happened to know who was the captain of her. The Emperor answered, 'Yes, and you would know him too when I tell you. Well, this is it. You said about four summers ago what a smart gig's crew I had in the *Meteor* after they had rowed us from her to your yacht *Iduna*. Well you know who was the bow-man.'

She said, 'Yes, I remember.'

'Well' said the Emperor, 'that is the same bow-man that is captain of the *Polly*, and was captain of that Yankee Wonder Boat last year, 1902.' She said to the steward to tell me personally she was glad I had got on, and she said, 'Wish him further success from me, do not forget.'

But I am sorry to have to say that motor cars was just getting all the rage and the owner told me the Emperor thought that motor cars would be the thing in war time, and later would he form motor-car clubs all over Germany, and when he had done that, would he form a tour to go with as many as he could get to go on the tour all over Europe? He would have to give up yachting for a time. Well that is what I have been thinking about a lot, in view of the things that has happened since, as you will see and put together yourself. The Emperor wanted to be the first of any thing that would help in warfare. So of course I was finished in Germany, or thought I was.

Anyway, I was paid off, so when I got home, I told the wife I would see if I could get a job as skipper of an English yacht the next summer.

So this ends 1903, with me writing all over the country for jobs. All the answers I could get were: 'Will file your testimonies for future reference.' So that's that, what!

9
More Racing in Germany

*Now Captain Diaper have you
Ever Said these words "I will Sink the Bloody "Iris"
before the Summer is over
I said No Sir I have not said
those words.*

So now for the doing of 1904, out of work and no signs of
getting any, but all our family had a good enjoyable Christmas.
I had brought home with me from Germany a round musical
contrivance that you could clamp a Christmas tree on the top of
it, wind it up and it would go round and round with music, or
without music, carrying a tree up to the weight of 150 pounds.
We had invited all our friends' children to the number of 24,
and it was a pretty sight with the tree dressed up, with Chinese
lanterns lit up and the other lights in the room turned out. It
looked very pretty and we had an enjoyable evening.

After Christmas I kept trying for a skipper's job till it came
on to March, 1904, when I secured a job as skipper of a 57-ton
yawl, Iris[1], laid up at Fay's Yard, Northam, what is now Camper
& Nicholson's. This yacht was owned by a Mr Conway Lloyd, of
Swansea, South Wales. We started to fit her out and make ready
for the summer. She was of a very old type and required a lot of
work to get her fixed up. I had the same crew of English sailors
and cook-steward as I had in Germany with me on the Polly. We
got her ready by the end of May, the owner joining us the 1st of
June, 1904.

Tom, Fanny and their children, L–R: Lilian, Florence (back), Violet (front), baby Tom, Fanny. Taken circa 1900.

We cruised about inside the Isle of Wight till the 1st of July. Then we started for Swansea; we were to do it in easy stages. Our first call was Weymouth and we arrived there with a very light wind at midnight, let go our anchor outside the harbour, and made all secure. We set anchor watch for the rest of the night, and in the morning the owner went on shore, asking me to go along with him. When we returned on board and talked with Mrs Lloyd, they decided to go in the harbour and stay there a week. We got under way, sailed in and moored to buoy moorings. After being there two days they said, as they liked it there, they would stop two weeks. It was the third day of our stay when the unexpected happened. I had a telegram from my wife to say she had an urgent telegram from Germany for me. Should she send it on? I asked the owner's permission to go and wire to her to do so, and it was granted. When I had got back and aboard Mr Lloyd had a yarn with me. He had already read my testimony. He said, 'Do you think it's from your late owner?' I said I thought so, or it might be from the designer Oertz. Well it came and it was from my last owner Buxenstein, asking me if I could go over to Berlin at once as he needed me and to wire to let him know if I could or not. He urgently needed me, so of course Mr and Mrs Lloyd listened to all I wanted and wished. I wired Berlin and asked him how long did he think he would need me for. He wired back '12 months.'

It must have been the way I acted and spoke, for Mr Lloyd said, 'Captain, I am afraid you want to go.'

'You has said it, sir,' says I, 'but what about you? I shipped with you. Is it too late for me to leave you?'

He asked as to the wages and suchlike. Well the wages was low. I told him I ought to get three times as much as I was getting. So he answered, 'Well, I won't stand in your way. If you can go home and find a man to take your place I will let you go willingly.'

So I promised I would leave first train in the morning. Well I left, arriving home in time for the men in Thornycrofts' to get home for dinner. There was a chum of mine I had in mind. So I saw him and shipped him, telling him to await till he saw me

again. So back I went from Southampton to Weymouth, saw
Lloyd and got my pay, when he asked if the new skipper was
a man my size. I said he was much bigger. I was sorry but my
uniform would be too small for him. 'Well,' says Lloyd, 'that can't
be helped. You tell him to get measured for his at the tailor's.' So
all was settled that way.

* * *

I wired Berlin, and I had a return wire saying, 'Bring your brother
along if possible. I am racing *Klein Polly*. I have wired passage
money for both.' Well I got my brother John and the money. I had
to take my brother straight to the Müggelsee Yacht Yard, set him
on getting the *Klein Polly* ready, then go back to Mr Buxenstein's
Berlin office, and then hear what he really wanted me for. When
we met he said, 'Well Diaper, I will tell you a story, and at the
end of it you will see what made me send for you. This is it. The
Emperor sent for me and told me to buy a yacht, and get a German
crew, all Germans except for one Italian who could speak many
languages. He told me to send the yacht to the Mediterranean,
and cruise along the Dalmatian coast, the Turkish coast, all around
the Adriatic, up as far as Salonica, and all around Italy. But, first
to send the yacht to Lusin Piccolo, where you can have the yacht
refitted. When ready send her to Fiume where you can join her in
February, about the 8th of that month, starting your cruise from
there. That, Diaper, is what I had to do. So, I bought the yacht,
got the crew, and she left the Elbe for the voyage out, but two
days after she had left, she returned to Cuxhaven with the captain
ill. So I engaged another skipper, and he came back four days
after leaving, saying he would not take a yacht like that across the
North Sea. So of course he left. So as not to be done I engaged a
third German captain. He said he would get her out there, but he

has proved no better than the others. He did cross the North Sea and put in at Lowestoft, but would not take her out to Gibraltar. So that is the reason I had sent for you by the sanction of the Kaiser. So now I ask you!'

I was going to answer him when he said, 'Wait and listen to what else I have to say. You must not say "yes" yet, for if you would take her I would want you to have a good trial with her first. You could take her as far as the Land's End if you thought she needed that much. After the trial then you could give me your answer. How is that?' I answered, 'I will try her, sir.'

'Now Diaper, where shall I tell that man to take her to, so that you can join her, and try her? You have got a free hand with her. The Emperor says you are the man that will do it and show our Germans up. So get on with it, captain.' His secretary, Mr Belitz, then wrote out a telegram as I told him. This is it: 'Tell him to get under way, weather permitting, and take the yacht to Southampton, but if too much wind in the Channel, put in at Dover and wait for new captain. If weather permits, you are to carry on to Southampton, but signal Dover if you do so, and send wire of arrival at either place you arrive at.'

'That is all, sir,' I said. 'But why Southampton?' he asked. 'Well after the trial I can get everything in the yachting line done with the least delay, after I have seen what is needed for such a trip.'

'All right Diaper. The order about *Vesta*[2] (that is the yacht's name) is yours.'

'Now this is Tuesday, sir. I will have *Klein Polly* on Wannsee Lake tomorrow, and return here at this office tomorrow, and go to the Friedrichstrasse Bahnhof to catch the midnight train from there with your secretary for Essen. From there I will go to Flushing, and he will go on to Paris. We both will meet at Dover. If the yacht has passed on our arrival, we will go straight on to London and Southampton.'

Well we did all this in a week. When we arrived at Dover, we found the yacht had passed on to Southampton, but we arrived at the Southampton Dock Station Friday at 5 o'clock. I had left that station at 5 o'clock the Friday before.

The secretary said as we parted, he for Radley's Hotel, me in a cab for Woolston and home: 'Well hustled, Captain Diaper, to have done as you have done in a week! We meet tomorrow at 10am. Have the yacht ready for sailing at 11am is your orders, captain. Well goodbye till tomorrow.'

September 1st, 1904. After a good night's rest I arrived at Radley's Hotel at 10am. The secretary told me he had found the yacht was there and he had seen the captain, and gave him my orders. The captain said the yacht would be ready at 11am. So the secretary bought some postcards and we went on board, and got under way at 11am. There was a very strong wind from the south-east. We tacked all the way out in a strong flood tide; the wind being against the tide made a nasty sea. We got as far as the Nab Light, when the secretary said his wife was seasick, and he felt like it himself, so I ordered the crew to turn the yacht round and keep her north-west. I went and looked for leaks and faults and booked all things to be done for the voyage.

When we had got into smoother water, me, the secretary and the German captain were together when the secretary said, 'Your answer, Captain Diaper; have you tried her enough for your satisfaction?' I replied, 'I have tried her enough, and will take her on the voyage and bring her back again.' 'Well, captain, I will wire to Mr Buxenstein to that effect as soon as I land.'

So the *Vesta* passed from a German trial of three German skippers, to an English skipper with German crew.

We sailed her into the River Itchen opposite my home. The secretary went on shore to return to Germany, taking the German captain with him. As he left he wished me bon voyage, and said he would be seeing me the next February at Fiume, Austria.

1905   We stayed a week at Southampton, and had the decks caulked and paid. We had a storm square sail made, skylight covers, and battens for hatchway, and lots of minor jobs attended to.

Now I think it will take too long to describe everything that happened on that trip – all but one or two incidents. But I can say from the time the owner came on board, till the time he left us six weeks later, the number of places we called in, always sailing, was 76 places in six weeks.

The incidents that occurred on this trip on the passage home happened this way. The German mate was unsatisfactory, and was sent home, the owner paying his passage, and giving him £10 extra. I think that was what led up to what occurred at Gibraltar. I had put the second mate up to first mate, and shipped an Austrian seaman to make up our complement of crew. This German who became first mate was big – 6 feet 2 inches in height, and big with it, and always grousing.

We called at Gibraltar, and I went on shore with the steward. He to get provisions, and myself to clear the ship's papers.

When I had finished and returned on board, I found all the crew drunk. I just had time to seize the owner's revolver and aim at a man who had a sailor down on the deck. He had a sheath knife. I shouted, 'Drop that knife or I will shoot you, Fritz.' I would have shot him, if he had not. So I picked up the knife, and when I had got them sobered up, they came to me, and all but the Italian and Austrian wanted to be paid off. The Germans did not want to cross the Bay of Biscay. They thought they would be paid off, and passage paid to get home, and £10 present.

I went and saw the German Consul, to see if he could get another crew. The order from Berlin was to put them in jail for mutiny and ship another crew. So I put the ship under police patrol, tried to ship another crew, but could not. When they heard I was trying for another crew, they said they would behave, and help take the ship home.

I had already wired to Berlin to send a sharp wire to the mate to read to the crew. So I having won, we had a week at Gibraltar. Then we left and we arrived at Southampton without further trouble, for the wire was to the effect that I had forgiven them, but at the least sign of mutiny again, I had orders from Germany to shoot on sight. Anyhow, all went well.

I stopped at Southampton for to have four days' leave, my brother taking my place, to go to Kiel.

* * *

I had only one week's leave, then I had a wire to go to Krupps Yard to show them the way to make a goose-neck iron connection for the racing boom. We was altering her rig from a yawl to a cutter for racing. Anyway the yard presented me with 200 marks, equal to an English ten pounds in them days.

There is another piece. Everywhere we went I went with the owner, and he was 'snap-shooting' everything. So I said, 'You seem to be taking a lot of snap-shots. What are you doing that for?' He replied, 'I am combining business with pleasure. I am making a tourist book for the Germans when they want to tour Europe. I shall do the same when we start the motor-car tour.'

Now there is one item I must mention. The Germans had built four 16-metre yachts. That was the class I was racing against with the *Vesta*. Earlier in the regattas, one of their captains had spoken to me in this way. 'Ah, Tom Diaper, you will not get so many prizes this year.' I answered, 'Why?' He said, 'We have one very fast boat, and besides Captain Begits of our Navy is sailing her.' Now Captain Begits I knew, for he raced with me on board the

Virginia II, and I respected him very much. So the words I answered were, 'Well, if I can beat the yacht *Iris*[3] – that was her name – I shall be beating the best boat, and the best man at the game you have got in Germany.'

We had reached Travemünde, and I was just going to turn in. The owner had been to the Yacht Club, for we were racing there the next day. The owner said he had a bone to pick with me, but he would let it stay till the morning. So when the morning came, all our class were moored up together in one bunch. The boss came on deck. He called out loud, 'Listen everyone of the 16-metre class. I am asking my captain a question, and that question concerns someone else in the class.' Turning to me, he said, 'Now Captain Diaper, have you ever said these words? "I will sink the bloody *Iris* before the summer is over."' I said, 'No, sir, I have not said those words.' 'Well,' said my boss out loud, 'Captain you has got to be at the Club at 9 o'clock, and the man that heard you say it will be there too, if he can hear me. I wish to clear this.' He then said, 'Is there anyone you wish to be present, skipper?' I said, 'Yes. Will you call out for the captain of the yacht *Hubertus*[4] to be there as well.' So he called out that, and the captain answered he would. So we raced that day, we winning first prize.

That evening we appeared at the Club, my boss telling me there was a talk of turning me out of Germany, but the Emperor and he – my owner – would be there. So we were all ready at the Club when I was called before them all, then the spokesman said, 'Did you say those words?' I said, 'Stop! Will you call Captain Hulberg of the *Hubertus*?' They called him in, and turning to the spokesman, I said, 'Sir, will you repeat those words I was supposed to have said.'

So he said, 'Now, Captain, this is what you was supposed to say: "I will sink the bloody *Iris* before the summer is over."'

I said, 'No, sir, definitely no, sir. Now may I ask Captain Hulberg a question?'

'Yes you may.'

'Well, Captain Hulberg, will you answer truthfully if I said those words when we had that chat some time ago?'

'No, captain, you did not say those words, and I do not believe you would ever say them.'

I said, 'Can you repeat the words I said about the *Iris*?'

He answered, 'Yes, captain; that if you could beat the *Iris* you would beat the best boat and man we had at the game in Germany.'

I answered, 'I have not seen you, or spoken to you since?'

'No, captain, we have not spoken since that time.'

My boss then spoke up. He said, 'What would you do, Captain Diaper, if you knew the man who would accuse you of saying them?'

'Me? Well, Sir, I would make him eat those words, or give him a good hiding.'

They had a conflab, the Emperor, my boss and the Yacht Committee, and then my boss laid down the law, and said that he would stop the slandering of Captain Diaper's character. He had orders that if he heard of any more slander to Captain Diaper's character, he was to take proceedings, and stop all sport for them, and he would do it too. So it ended up, and we ended the summer by winning the Ladies' Prize at Swinemünde.

When we laid the yacht up at Kiel, I had a month's holiday, but I was not to go out of Germany. The boss told me to send for my wife. I did, and I met her at Hamburg. We had ten days there sightseeing, and then spent the rest of the time at Kiel, seeing everything of note there was to be seen.

Then the time came to send her home from Hamburg, while I went on to Berlin, and raced *Klein Polly* on the inland lakes. After taking ten first prizes, we laid her up and had a month standing by to take *Vesta* to Norway. But after waiting two weeks, they decided to leave the *Vesta* at Kiel, then to send a Norwegian crew for her the next spring. So that finished me, and I returned to home. I cannot write any more about *Vesta*. I should not find a book large enough to put it all in. So goodbye *Vesta* and 1905 – another gone.

* * *

We now come to 1906.

In the spring of this year I had a letter from Mr Oertz to know if I would take charge of a 15-metre yacht for a Captain Wydle of Hamburg. So I done as always by drawing up an agreement, and getting the thing signed by all parties before I would leave England, the only difference being we would sign for daily pay, instead of weekly or monthly, for he was a German mercantile captain. They used to cheat the German crew of a day's pay in some months, such as if you signed on for monthly pay, some months had 30 days, and some had 31, but when it came to pay up, I know of some who would say you signed up monthly, and it is universal at sea that you sign for 30 days to the month. So by getting paid by the day I would have no trouble. So I got the agreement duly signed by myself, the owner, and the secretary of the Kiel Yacht Club.

We went over in May, and raced the season at the top of the class in winning 20 firsts and two seconds.

One day at Kiel we had an admiral of the German Navy on board to race with us. They did not know I understood German as much as I did, for I hardly ever spoke to him in German. The admiral was telling the boss in German that I did not sail the boat as she should be sailed. So I spoke to him in German, and told him that if he spoke that way again, I would turn the yacht around, and anchor, and take my crew home to my own country, which was more than he had another country to go to. Anyhow he bowed, and salaamed, and asked to be forgiven.

There was a photo of the most dangerous start ever made in Germany. The admiral brought one on board for me to see. He gave me 40 marks when he left, and thanked me for the sport I had made, and for frightening everyone aboard the committee boat, for they thought I was going to cut her in two. I think all the Germans were frightened, for my old boss's secretary was on board, and saw it all. He said the same; it was the most daring thing he had seen me do. Anyway that start put me five minutes ahead of the rest. I had done it without infringing any of the rules. Anyhow we came out on top of our class.

When the yacht was laid up at Travemünde, I sent the crew home, and I went to the inland lakes to *Klein Polly* and was the top of the tree again. I paid off, and returned home wondering what would be the next boat I should have, although the owner had asked me if I would come back to the *Carola*[5], that was the name of Captain Wydle's yawl. I told him I would if I had nothing to do.

So that finished 1906.

Early in the spring of 1907, I had a letter from Captain Wydle to say he was sorry that he would not be wanting me as the Emperor ordered him to have all German sailors on board the *Carola* that season. About a week after I had a letter from Oertz the designer, to ask me to go over to Hamburg and take charge of an 8-metre what he was building for Mendelssohn the banker. I went over and he told me she would become very fast. When I saw her I was disappointed in her. He told me he had a different design for her. I pointed out her faults as I saw them. He would not alter her and we nearly had a row. Well I told him I would do my best and when she was ready took her to the inland lakes.

We raced two times and with only two boats. We lost the first race and would have lost the second race, only the other boat ran on the mud and could not get off. So we got in and took the first prize. The new yacht was a complete failure. The owner asked me to wire to Oertz to come to the next races and race on board, so he could see for himself what was the fault of her not going well. We only took one more prize by a fluke.

As he, the designer, would not come and race in her at Kiel week, we packed her up and sent her back to the yard and her designer, and we fitted out his old 8-metre. We raced her in the remaining nine races, getting eight first prizes and getting three extras, making 11 firsts. We lost the one race owing to the wind failing.

Mr Mendelssohn said, 'Well, Captain Diaper, I hope our sending the new *Kranick II*[6] back to Oertz will not hurt you in your career, but I should think he could see it was not your fault, as you fitted out *Kranick* I, and she eight years old, and taking all the prizes in her.' 'Well, sir,' I said, 'that of course is the way of the world. You never can tell.' He thanked me very much. We laid *Kranick* I up in a yard close to Potsdam, and I returned home, still hoping I should get a good yearly job yet.

So that ends my yachting of 1907.

I had been told to have only winning flags. I was not to lose; in any case, I should get no losing money.

For the remainder of 1907 and the start of 1908 I tried, and wrote to everywhere I could think of, to get a start yachting, for there was getting less English in the German yachts and more Germans taking to it, but a funny thing happened.

The owner of the *Carola* what I was with, wrote to me in the spring of 1908 to say the German sailors was no good in yachts and could get no prizes, and would I come and take charge of *Carola* that summer. So not being able to get a yacht in England, I went to Germany. Again and again I showed the Germans how to win prizes. In my old ship the *Carola* I ended up by being the top of the class again, so I will end this by putting in a copy of the testimony the owner sent to me.

Copy of Testimony.

The undersigned do hereby certify that Captain Thos. Diaper has served on board my Cruiser Yacht, the Yawl 'Carola' of 41 tons, as Sailing Master for two seasons. During this time I had the best of opportunities to watch him, and I can safely say that I never found anybody who kept his quietness in trying circumstances as he does.

The starts he made were simply perfect and were fully appreciated by all who saw the 'Carola' start. I can, with a good conscience, recommend Captain Diaper to anyone requiring a perfect Sailing Master for his yacht. He leaves my services as I have sold the 'Carola' to a gentleman in Copenhagen.

Hamburg, 28th March, 1909.   *Signed: L Wydle*

10
A Theatrical Owner

a fisherman had found our small Boat intact a Lloyds Official Told me I had caught the atlantic cable and was up setting all messages But anyway I proved him wrong.

Year 1909. As I was not able to get a job as a yacht skipper on my own boat, my brother who was acting as boatswain in the Ferry Yacht Yard owned by a Mr McDonald, asked me if I would care to work in there as they had got a Government contract and they wanted someone who could do the rigging Government fashion. So I took on the job. In between the jobs of rigging, I took on run jobs to go anywhere they wanted, to take boats from one port to another as required. So I went to Amsterdam and fetched over from there to Portsmouth two of Pickford's motor transport boats, what do the trading around the ports inside the Isle of Wight.

Then in August a Mrs Shaw-Storey had chartered the Yard's steam yacht *Sea Snake*[1], and I took that job as skipper of her for the time.

After that I stayed at work at the Ferry Yard till it came to January, 1910. Then the manager, Mr J Neill came and asked me if I would go to Waterford, Ireland, and take a 1,000-ton barge from there to Limerick on the north-west of Ireland. I told him I would, then he told me the story about her.

She was built on the Thames. She had a Kroumout Diesel engine, and I had to go to London to a shipping firm in Fenchurch Street, for they was the real firm for the job. First to try it was the pilots of the Shannon. They came from there to London to take her from there to the Shannon, but when they got her to Portland Bill, something went wrong, and a naval man-of-war towed them into Weymouth. They had to return and would not take her any further. Then Mr J Neill sent a captain and two in crew to Weymouth to take her to the Shannon.

Well, the cause of him to ask me was, when they had got her within 50 miles of the Irish coast, her crew had got the scare. They must have been badly frightened, for they turned around, and ran the red ensign up the mast-head upside down, and that meant they was in distress.

A large fishing steam trawler saw them, put a tow-line on board, and towed them to Waterford on the south-east coast of Ireland. The skipper of the barge did not ask the trawler what he would tow him to Waterford for or how much, so the result was that the trawler was suing the barge owners for salvage. They told me they wanted her got to Limerick as soon as I could get her there.

So I went to the shipping firm in London then travelled to Fishguard and caught the night boat for Rosslare, Ireland, arriving at Waterford on the Thursday and caught the boat for Passage West Friday morning.

The man acting as mate was an old shipmate and neighbour of mine, and he was gladly surprised to see me. Being Friday, I said to him, 'Tom, I will, if I can, make next Tuesday, weather permitting, the day to leave. Meanwhile, we will just go steady along and see that we have everything aboard. And the motor-man, he is a man from the motor firm of Norris & Henty's where the Kroumout motor was made, the first of its kind to be built in

England, and they want that motor to take her to Limerick under her own power.'

The Tuesday morning came and we left; no wind, calm sea, smooth as glass, the motor-man having said that he had everything he wanted for the trip on board, compressed air and all. Well we had been running about one and a half hours when one cylinder split right through the middle. We just managed to get to a small place and, having spares on board, worked the rest of the day and night to get a new one replaced by 8 o'clock am. I was just going to the post office to wire the event, as I had to do, when the motor-man came to me and asked, 'How far are we going to Queenstown?' '80 mile' I answered. He said, 'I don't think I have enough air for that far.'

'Well,' I said, 'we have started on this trip and I don't go back to where I left. I am going to the post office and will wire London to send three bottles to Queenstown. I have been here four days; now we have started, you tell me this and I don't like it. I shall never turn back. Queenstown is the only place we can receive the air by train or boat. If I got to put in a small place like this they would have to send it by road with horse and cart, and that would delay us too much.'

So we got ready to start as soon as I returned. The weather looked like turning and I wanted to get to a safe harbour, for this one is not. So I done the post and left, reaching Queenstown entrance just on night. We entered and was a half mile away from the town when the motor conked out. We had to let go anchor and await for the air.

Well, we was a week waiting for the air. While we were waiting I asked the motor-man to have everything ready. He said he wanted some new copper piping. He and me went on shore to hunt for some. We could not get it. We was just going to go back on board when a man accosted me saying, 'Are you from that motor barge off there?' he says, 'Is the captain on board or ashore? I thought she was at Passage West still.'

I replied, 'I am the skipper.'

'But' he said, 'this man had a very heavy black moustache and we agreed that I should come to Passage West and tow him to Limerick for £280. That is my tow-boat lying there.'

'Well, captain,' says I, 'that man was ill and was recalled to London and I was sent over here to take the barge for Waterford under her own power. No tow for me, thank you.'

Well, we got the bottle of air, then, getting a fine day, left Queenstown for Crookhaven, County Cork. We had a good day's run along the south coast of Ireland, slipped inside the Fastnet Rock, arriving at Crookhaven just at dusk, with a heavy westerly gale and the Atlantic sea and rollers getting up quick. After we had anchored, the natives said sometimes they could just see a spot on the sea and the exhaust mingling with it. They could not make out what kind of a boat it was. Anyway, we was forced by the gales of wind to stop at Crookhaven just over three weeks. Then there came one fine day and we started for St Vincent, 50 mile from Crookhaven. I went inside most of the western rocks and there are plenty on the west coast of Ireland. Half way we had run when the motor-man said we would have to go back as the main bearing was getting too hot. Now I says, 'Not back.' I had told him it was just the same distance to go on. 'Try to keep them cool,' I said. We just managed to do it when the motor stopped on its own. I borrowed a set of chain blocks to lift the motor off its bearings, when another Atlantic gale arrived. We drove and our anchor caught the Atlantic cable, for that is where it lands from America on this side of the Atlantic. Our stern was just clear of the rocks. We were short of food, our boat – small boat I mean – had broke away. We heard after that the lifeboat's crew was stood by 48 hours. When the worst was over – about 60 hours of it – the gale abated and we got ashore. The first thing was a good feed. A fisherman had found our small boat intact. A Lloyds official told me I had caught the Atlantic cable, and was upsetting all messages, but anyway I proved him wrong.

The weather was getting better, our motor having been put right, we left there and ran to the mouth of the Shannon just as another westerly sprang up. We anchored for the night under the lee of the island at the entrance. At daylight the next morning we got under way and steamed up the Shannon. We had got three-quarters of the way up the river when a pilot boat stopped us and put a pilot aboard. He asked me where the other pilot was that was to board me at the mouth of the Shannon, and bring me up the river. I said, 'I have seen no sign of a pilot.' He says, 'I can hardly believe that, because there are two pilots at the mouth of the river on the look-out for you.' I replied, 'Ask the crew.' He did, and of course they said 'No.' Anyhow he got us up to Limerick and docked us just before dark, the tide serving.

So the next morning the owner came on board, and I put the barge through several tests in the dock, putting at full speed all out on the motor for the dock wall straight ahead, and putting her into reverse, the motor-man acting promptly. We finished up without mishap. They were well pleased with what I had done, and said I ought to have had command in the first place as the distance I had brought her in five days' run, was the distance the first crew and the second crew had taken six months to do. They presented me with a month's extra pay, so I left for London crossing Ireland by rail to Dublin, and from Kingstown to Holyhead by boat, then to the shipping office in London. They were well pleased, and they also gave me an extra month's pay. I returned to Southampton having been gone six weeks. It only took five days' motoring, all the other time was the worst gales that had been known for a good number of years. Well after all said and done, 'All's well that ends well.'

* * *

It was getting on to the end of March, 1910, when I returned to my work in the Ferry Yard[2]. I had been at work there for some time when they lent me again to the shipping firm to go to Amsterdam to take the third motor packet boat from there to Portsmouth. I forgot to mention that I was to have a five pound bonus if I brought the boats direct from the place I had to take them to, without going into any port on the way. Three trips I had made for the Pickford's boats I had made direct, although two of them was pretty rough weather. I returned to the Yard again. Then the owner Mr McDonald asked me to get a crew, and go to Exmouth in the West Bay and get *Kathlinda*, a steam yacht of 70 tons, and bring her to the Ferry Yard. He had bought her, so I went, and in a week was back at the Yard with her.

The Yard hands was fitting out a 30-ton yawl, the Government work being finished for the time being. I was sent to help them in the fitting out of her. One day I was told the owner was coming, and he would ask for me. Then he appeared and asked me a lot of questions about the yawl and when I told him she was a sister to the boat what the American, Captain Slocum, sailed around the world in, he asked me if I would sail her around the world. I said I would. So I shipped with him as skipper of the yawl on the understanding that we would make Hamble our home port on moorings close to a house-boat he had there also, and he would use the yawl at weekends to sail about inside the Isle of Wight with actors and actresses he would bring down from his theatre in London.

Well we had carried on like that for about a month. He had a young housekeeper. I termed her a young cat. She had a very violent temper, and she tried it out on me one day. That is how I found out she was not English, for she had used up all her English in her temper. When she started in another lingo I said something, and then I said, 'Ich ist nich schweinerie.' Then you should have seen her! Someone asked what was it I had said. 'Well,' I said, 'I answered her back in her own language that she was using on me. It was German, for in English she called me a pig, and I would not stand that from my own countrymen, and certainly not from a German fraulein.' Then the boss asked me to go forward till he had quieted her, and then we went for a sail.

It was two weeks after that we had orders to be ready for a sail at 10 o'clock. At 10.30am the boss paddled from the house-boat to us, and when he got on board he said, 'We shall not be sailing today. I have bad news from London, I am broke. How long will it take you to lay this yacht up, and moor her in a mud berth?' I said, 'Two weeks from now.' 'Very well,' he said, 'I shall catch the 3pm train to London. I will pay you the two weeks' money before I go,' and he thanked me for what I had done, and said he would send me a testimony from London. He added, 'You and Madam "X" is friendly now we are leaving. You know she is a great singer, and sings for charity.' I answered, 'She can sing better than she can make a row.'

So that ended the voyage around the world.

* * *

I returned to the Ferry Yard and worked through the winter up to March, 1911, then a gentleman asked me to fit out the Kathlinda[3] the 70-ton steam yacht I had brought to the yacht yard from Exmouth. I fitted her out between other jobs of Government till June, then went cruising about the South Coast till after the regattas inside the Isle of Wight. Then he asked me to take her to Scotland, and pick him up at Rothesay. He joined us with a party at the end of August, and we cruised about the lochs till we reached Oban. Then, making that our home port, we used to go out for a cruise, taking friends of theirs daily, till the middle of September. Then we were going to work our way further north.

He wanted me to take her everywhere without a pilot. We reached Loch Leven when he said, 'Skipper we will have a look at this loch.' So we entered, getting about three-quarters up the loch when it looked doubtful. The chart we had showed no passage-way further up, so I stopped her altogether. I could see a large steam yacht further up the loch. The owner came on the bridge saying, 'What are you stopping for?' I said to him, 'To make sure of the right channel.' He replied, 'You are all right as long as you are in the centre of the loch. I was up here last year,' and he rang the telegraph full speed ahead. We increased speed to ten knots, when keeping a sharp look-out, I saw a stick with a salmon tin stuck on the top. I had my hand on the telegraph and rang, 'Stop. Full Speed Astern'; at the same time the boss was calling my attention to some people getting a stag on board of a launch. Just as he said, 'What did you ring the telegraph for?' I said, 'For this!' Up we came from 8 fathoms of water on to 2 feet of water, and being a very narrow boat we fell sharply over to port, and just missed the stick on the port side. It was a good job we were that far inside the stick. If we had been ten feet further to port we should have turned turtle into the private dredged channel what I learned of after, when the mate of the steam yacht *Jason*[4] – the yacht up the loch – came to ask if they could give us any help.

Our people left in a hurry the next day. The crew of the *Jason* came, and we passed a wire under her lower side, and made it fast to our hawse pipe, by reeving a 2-inch wire through them, and through the eye in the end of his 6-inch salvaging wire, leaving the whole coil in the boat. I sounded over the stern 8 fathoms. Twelve feet further in there was only 1 foot, 6 inches. The tide was high water at 7am and we could walk nearly all around her all day. The Scotch people at the farm close by were very good to us, bringing us milk, eggs, etc.

The steam yacht came down the loch and moored straight off from us on the lower side of the point we were aground on. We rowed the wire on board of her ready for high water at 7.30pm. We had passed a 5-inch Manila hawser through our aperture to keep the steel one in position, and I was to be the only one on board, standing by with a sharp axe to cut the Manila rope as soon as we were off, so we could swing around head on to the other yacht. Well at 7.30pm the signal was all ready, all our crew was off in our boats. I shouted, 'All ready, sir.' He started to heave on his bow anchors, and our yacht started a foot or two. I hailed, 'She is moving. Full speed, captain.' Then he started his engines, heaving his anchors at the same time, and off we went like a train. When I chopped the rope she turned like a top, and smothered me with spray. It went off without any accident, and we anchored for the night, and turned in at 10pm having found she had not made any water.

On getting out of my bunk at 5am next morning, I trod in water. It reached to my knees. The strong running tide in the night must have washed away the seaweed what had filled the cracks where she, in falling over, had cracked four of her bottom plates, that we could not inspect under her boilers. What we found after was that we could not light up our own boilers, as the water was above the fire. The other yacht's crew with all their hand pumps and we with our own got the water down till we could light up, and get steam. Our own pumps could then just keep the water under the stoke-hole plates.

Having wired the yacht yard on Kerry Island to have the slip ready, the *Jason* towed us the 30 miles back. We was hauled straight up on the slipway, and found on surveying her under water the port side, that four plates were badly cracked and buckled. We had a court job with Lloyd's Insurance, someone trying to put the blame on me. Being told that I would never have charge of another yacht under Lloyd's Insurance, I asked them what they had done to Lord Charles Beresford, Commander-in-Chief of the British Navy, as he was the last one before me to get on the same place with his yacht, and he had to get shipwrights and launch his yacht.

I left my log in their charge after I reached home, and told the owner I was finished. I had letters and charts sent me by the Admiralty and Lloyd's Agency to mark out the exact position the *Kathlinda* struck and laid, draw the position she laid in, and why I called it Dog Nose point.

After reading my log I was exempted from all blame, and if ever I want to command another ship they would get me one.

Later on the owner sold the steam yacht, and I got a job as rigger at the Ferry Yard on the Government side work that was done there again.

The end of the *Kathlinda* job. So this ends 1911.

1912. I continued to work in the yard trying all the time for to get a ship so that I could go to sea again, but without success till May, 1912. I heard that a yacht agency had opened up in the High Street, Southampton, so I went and saw the official there, and this copy of the testimony below shows the nature of the job I took.

I employed Captain Diaper in May, 1912, to bring round my 80-ton yacht 'Witch[5]' from Kingstown, Ireland, to Gosport. Very heavy weather and fog was experienced. In spite of this, the boat arrived without a scratch.

I was very pleased with his careful handling of the boat, and the manner in which the contract was carried out.

ACH Dean, Captain, RGA

3rd June, 1912

11
1914. Too Old at 45

So I answered this way if you can believe a Man who Since we have been here has drank has much as 4 Bottles of Whiskey besides Rum. Every evening and is now Drinky with the D. T's I will warn you that you will be sorry That you ever had any Dealings with him,

I had only been home a day from the *Witch's* trip, when I received a letter from Captain Wydle, my boss of the German yacht *Carola*. He wanted me to go to Germany as captain, and bring my own crew with me for the yacht of a friend of his, who was his guest on board of the *Carola* the time I had charge of her. So as I knew the gentleman, I wired I would, for when we were on the *Carola* he promised that I should be his captain if ever he had a yacht.

1912

I was vacant at the time, and he said it would be a better and longer job than the *Carola*. This yacht was a 60-ton cruising ketch, but as he had promised me it would be better, I shipped a crew of six, and went over.

On arriving, I found she was laid up at Travemünde in the Baltic, and that her owner was a Swiss, a big manufacturer at Zurich, the capital of Switzerland. The yacht was the only Swiss vessel to fly the Swiss flag on salt water.

Well we made her ready in quick time, and we had not been sailing in the Baltic more than two weeks, than I knew by then I should not like his ways of yachting, for he wanted to do his sailing at night time from place to place. Then in day time, in harbour, have workmen on board altering things to his liking, and keeping the crew always busy.

We cruised about the Baltic July and August. In September he decided to take the yacht to England, and there try to exchange the yacht and the rest in money for a much larger sailing ketch.

While we were crossing the North Sea, him and myself formed a plan for a voyage around the world. I could do no wrong in his eyes. I really thought I had a job for life, but as soon as we reached Southampton, he took to drink and give me and my crew the sack. He upbraided me before the manager of the yard we was laying at, the manager telling me I need not apply to him, or the yard for another ship or work. So I answered this way, 'If you can believe a man who since we have been here has drunk as much as four bottles of whisky, besides rum every morning, and is now "drinky" with the DT's, I will warn you that you will be sorry that you ever had any dealings with him.' So I left at that, the only yacht I had the sack from.

Three weeks later the same manager sent for me and told me he was sorry at what he had said to me. But I was right and he was sorry that he had any dealings with the Swiss.

* * *

So after finishing with the Swiss, I went to work in the Ferry Yard on my old job and kept it all the winter up till July, 1913, when I had a letter from a German gentleman, a Herr Wolters, to say he was bringing a German 15-metre, *Paula III*, to Southampton to be hauled up for a good clean up for the regattas inside the Isle of Wight. Would I take the job as pilot and get a slipway for her? So as the Ferry Yard was too full to do the work, I got a slipway at White Bros for her. I put in the job as pilot inside the Wight. During the Solent races we won about one flag more than the rest of the class. There were eight in the class with all the noted racing skippers of the day and they shared the winnings very evenly. I did not do bad. She went back to Germany and I went back to the Ferry Yard, to the same old job. 1913 ended.

* * *

This is 1914. Still at work in the Ferry Yard, doing the Government work till about May, when we fitted out a very old yacht, a yawl of about 25 tons. When we had her ready, Mr Beazley, a marine salvor, came to me and asked me to take the yacht with a man to help me and another man who was to go aboard and steer a small 16-ton Dutch yacht, the *Coo-ee*, what was laying dismasted at Weymouth. We were to go there, take her in tow and bring her back here to the Ferry Yard. I said I did not much like it; for a sailing boat to tow another was not very nice. Anyway we went. The Weymouth people had got her outside the harbour, so we took her in tow and sailed away with a nice breeze. When we got out of Weymouth Bay and off Swanage, it fell flat calm. We hauled alongside one another and had tea. Then I asked the others if we would draw lots to see who would stay on board the Dutchman; but Hemery said he was told by the boss to do it and he would – each one to the boat the boss had told him off to do.

It looked fine enough, but by midnight, about 2 miles from the Needles, it was blowing a living gale. We broke all the tow-lines, but we rounded her to, trying to pick the Dutch yacht up. But with the ebb tide coming through the Needles and a gale of wind against it, we could not have lost her in a worse place.

So we sailed as hard as we could for Yarmouth, Isle of Wight, to get the Totland lifeboat out. Me and my mate offered to help, but they could not let the lifeboat go as it was too rough; but they telephoned along the coast to keep a sharp look-out. So me and my mate was worrying – would people think we had run away and left her? But any good sailor who knows the Needles ebb tide with a westerly gale and thick with rain and only one man aboard a dismasted yacht, would have a think coming, if he thought he could pick her up without sinking one or both of them.

At 6am daylight we went on shore and found she had been sighted at the back of the Shingles in the Needles passage. At 8 o'clock the lifeboat, the *Robert Fleming*, could not row ahead – too much wind and sea. There was a Trinity steamboat at Yarmouth, so we got them to tow the lifeboat out to her. By 12 noon the steamboat came steaming back with the lifeboat and our Dutchman, with our mate on board. If any three men had a night of worry, we did. He thought we had sunk, for he saw us round to and give one plunge into a big sea and he thought we had gone down then and thought he had as good as gone too. But all's well that ends well. Thank God we did that day. I told Beazley I would never do it again – take a sailing boat outside the Isle of Wight to act as tow to a dismasted boat. We towed the Dutchman to the Ferry Yard the next day. After I had asked Beazley to tip the lifeboat men, he was fairly liberal to them. So he needed to be[1].

* * *

Still 1914. Beazley came to me on June the 10th to ask if I would take two hands and go down the Baltic Sea to a German port and bring a German 15-metre yacht from Travemünde back to the Ferry Yard. So I left with two hands in a German mail boat called *Cap Trafalgar*[2], the same ship as the Cunard liner called *Carmania*[3] sank in the First World War. They were both made armed cruisers.

The German ship landed us at Hamburg. Beazley was with us and did he have a surprise at the people who knew me and, when we got to Travemünde and Herr Slighting's Yacht Werft, the way the Herr and me was talking German together? He asked me how I would get on for money, as he could only let me have five pounds. But I said, 'You need not worry about that. You call on your way back at Kiel to Shutt and Sieck, ship chandlers. They will let me have any money up to one thousand pounds. You call there and mention Captain Diaper who was in *Polly*.' Well he left and it was three weeks before we could leave after, as they had so many yachts to get out of the way of the Nis[4] 16-metre.

We had very little wind when we did leave, but after we had rounded Fehmarn Island the wind came off the shore a hard gale and thick with rain. When about 15 miles from Kiel it was very dark and rainy. We had our own navigation lights burning brightly, when a fleet of torpedo boats appeared and started to see how close they could fire at us. I hailed them in German, but I got no answer. But they had a surprise coming later, for when I had run the distance by the log to Kiel lightship, we just sighted her with no lights showing. I said to my two mates, 'I reckon they are at manoeuvres and the lights are out there too. I am going into the mouth of the Canal.' They said, 'You will never do it.' 'All right,' I said, 'I will give you all a shock.'

So sure enough we made it, let go anchor and stowed the sails quick and turned in in the dark without seeing anything. I did not think I had been asleep long when I was awakened by one of my mates to say there was a German officer who wanted the captain. I said, 'Ask him to come aboard.'

Now in the saloon our light hung down from the skylight. It was hanging low over the table with a shade around it, so that when I stood up my face was in the shade. So as the German officer came into the cabin, I stood up to greet him. First words he said was, 'Good morning, captain. How did you get in here? You was not here at dark last night and it is only just got daylight now. Who brought you in? You are English.'

'No one brought me in, sir, only myself. I done it, sir.'

'Without any harbour lights showing?'

'Quite right, Captain Begits,' I answered, 'Captain Tom Diaper at your service, sir.' With that I sat down. Then he saw my face.

'Good God,' he said, 'it will be a bad day for Germany if Tom Diaper ever enters the British Navy; for we may shortly be at war, captain.'

'Well, sir,' I said, 'you have had something to do with my getting in here, for you showed me a lot when for three summers you was captain of the School of Soundings for torpedo boats and a guest on board of the yachts I was skipper of; and you represented the owner of the *Virginia II* when we raced together in the 8-metre class. You showed me a lot where you had been sounding, if you remember back, sir.' So we had a friendly chat about old times.

Then he said, 'Captain, I advise you to make all the speed you can to get home, for we are having our big manoeuvres and there is risk of war on France and England. I will see you get a quick tow through the Kiel Canal. After this do not appear to know me; but if I should have occasion to speak to you, you will know how to answer and I will give the usual sign. It is 7am. Now be ready to tow at 10am.'

'Very good, sir,' I replied. We shook hands and parted. That was the last I saw of him. We towed as arranged right through the Canal that day, reaching the Elbe end about 5 o'clock with the

German fleet of warships. Wanting some money, I decided to stay in the Canal, for there was a hard wind blowing from the west, as that would do for an excuse. I noticed on the sides of the men-of-war we passed that they all had lots of anchors, so I wanted to see what they had on the in, or shore, side of them. That was the only time I was ordered to keep away from a battleship. They had mines on deck on the shore side. So the next morning I found Shutt and Sieck's agent and telephoned to them at Kiel. When he heard who it was, he upbraided me for not calling on him at the Kiel end. I said I had not time and said I had no money. 'That means you want some. How much? A thousand pounds?'

'Not that much. Ten pounds in English will do.'

'All right. My agent will see that you get it today. Thank you, Tom, for sending Mr Beazley to me. Goodbye, Tom. Happy crossing to your home and respects to your wife and family.'

Next morning the harbour master came and told me that he had a telephone message from the admiral of the port of Kiel to tell me the wind was in our favour for crossing the North Sea. I took that tip and knew we should have to force her across. Well anyhow we had a good run across and got to the Ferry Yard on a Wednesday. On the next Sunday war was declared, August 4th, 1914.

So that was the last time I was in Germany. But the German fleet had left the Canal before we had. As we got out of the River Elbe and had just passed Heligoland, I saw the German fleet laying. I took particular notice and had just put my opera glasses away when a German torpedo boat sidled up to us, asking where we came from and where we were going. I answered him, but he accompanied us for a couple of hours, then he left us. So after I arrived home, I wrote to Whitehall to be put in charge of a minesweeper to go mine-sweeping at the mouth of the River Elbe, but I had answer to the effect that I was too old at 45. Also

I tried to get in charge of a mine-layer in Tate's Navy[5]; the same answer – too old at 45!

* * *

So it went on and the war went on. I worked on at the Ferry Yard, making wire ties for light equipment bridges what the yard was making. So I continued working for Beazley, only going to sea outside of the Isle of Wight in a small yacht what he converted into a steam tow-boat. I went out in her to pick up any patrol motor-boats what got disabled and had to be towed back to port to be repaired. This went on till 1915, April 20th, when I was fed up with the yard. I left and went with the sailor painters, till a chance came and I shipped as able seaman on board the *Minnesota*[6] trooping.

On 12th May, 1915, she was taking the troops and horses and guns and munitions from Southampton to Havre and Dieppe. One trip after we had discharged at Havre, I was at the wheel. We had just passed the last fairway buoy when I saw something at two cables away on our starboard side. It was a calm sea and you could see the ripple of the water it made going along. I called the captain's attention to it. It was a submarine, but he ordered me to zig-zag the course. The sub would not surface, for there were two French destroyers not far away. I steered a quick zig-zag course that gave him no chance to put a torpedo into us. Anyway we got clear away. Someone must have seen it, for when we got to Cowes, where we had to report and clean up for the next trip, a torpedo boat from Portsmouth called out as we were sailing the captain to shore: 'What ship do that boat belong to?'

The captain called out, '*Minnesota's* boat.'

The answer came: 'Everything all right, captain. You got away from that submarine all right then?'

'OK,' answered the captain.

I was asked after the war was over if I ever got the 20 pounds for reporting the first German sub I said 'No' and I did not. I knew many seamen in other troopers what said they all had letters sent on board of them, telling them that the man who first sighted a German sub would get 20 pounds like Diaper in the *Minnesota*. But if ever there were 20 pounds sent to the *Minnesota* for me, I swear I never received it.

Now there were in all a 100 or more transports laying at anchor round about Cowes, all taking their turn to go up to Southampton when called upon to take troops to France. The Cowes' town people got up a regatta for the transports' cutters for a series of points. Twenty points was the highest number of points to make. The boat that got that number of points first had won the splendid Town Cup, what the town had put up. Our skipper took me to see it and said, 'Diaper, I am putting our sailing cutter in the races. I should like to see that cup in my parlour and you are going to sail the boat for it. What do you think your chances are of winning it?'

1918

I replied, 'I will tell you, sir, after I have sailed the first race.'

Well, the day came for the race. We made a good start among the 30 boats what were there, and we finished first, taking the first four points for the first boat. So the skipper asked me to put him ashore, taking me to his hotel, gave me a drink and told me I was to go aboard and tell the chief officer to let all hands come ashore and Diaper was to get all aboard again by sunset. I went on the quay side and a lot was standing in a ring, when on the other side of the ring I saw a man I had seen in Germany. He had a false beard on but I knew him by the mark under his eyes. As soon as he saw me making through the crowd and our eyes met, he was off and disappeared in the crowd. I had spotted him and he knew I had too.

I must mention that in 1918 while I was working in Thornycrofts, I and my wife got on to the floating bridge at Woolston to cross to Southampton; it was crowded. Just as the bell rang at the Southampton side and the bridge stopped, I saw a man standing up in a car. I tried to get through the crowd. His eyes caught mine. It was the spy I had seen at Cowes some time before. But I was too late. The car started as I called 'Spy!' Everyone had to look out, but the car got away and no one noticed its number.

I can explain the spy. His name was 'X'. He was an artist painter who had been on three of the German yachts as guest of the owners. He told me he had run through two fortunes and was well connected in Germany. Three summers he raced in yacht racing in the Solent. Two summers he was in two-and-a-half-rater class and he represented the owner in the German 15-metre what I was pilot of one summer in the Solent. But he was a bit of a boozer. I was a bit sorry for him in a certain way, for he was a good friend to me in Germany and I brought him across the North Sea in the Swiss yacht from Germany to Southampton. At that time he told me where I should touch the mud, tacking against a head wind at low water in the River Itchen. It was between the Ray's coal jetty but closest the floating bridge; and the second time would be opposite Dibble's shipyard at Belvedere and that was correct, for that is where we did touch. So that was the man I could be sure of was the spy.

Returning to 1915, we were taken off the run from Southampton to France and ordered with 11 other transports to go to London. So we left Cowes for London and that finished our chance for the Cowes Town Cup, for everyone reckoned our boat would win it. The skipper was disappointed. When we was docked in London, all hands was paid off and I went home to Itchen Ferry.

12
Collision in the Channel

I got some Hurrican Lamps lit then Me and Cheif officer went to find out how much we had been damaged, I got down the fore peak ladder two rongs I was in water Could have rowed 2 boat through the hole in her bow

I had only been three days when they sent for me to rejoin the *Minnesota* again. So I went up to London on the 14th September, 1915, slept on board that night and signed on as AB and Lamps. The next day I had to have a police escort to take me to the shipping office. I did not know there was a strike on before I got there. After I had signed on, the police took me on board the ship. There I found the same boatswain and carpenter. I was glad there was someone I knew. They had not been paid off with us. We left London dock about the 18th, the shore gang getting her out of dock into the river. There the rest of the crew was brought off in a tug. And what a sample I had in the after end of the ship with the second officer to look after! Our crew in the starboard watch was a Finn, a Greek, a Yank and a Pole; and only the Yank we could understand. Of course the others had not entered the war yet; but one good thing, they were very good sailormen, understanding what had to be done. You only had to point and make motions with your hand and they knew what to do.

Well we got clear of the Thames without mishap and got in the English Channel. We understood we were going to America for munitions. We had got outside my back door, as I called it, off

St Catherine's Point, Isle of Wight, when it came on a thick fog all at once. In less than a quarter of an hour I heard the telegraph ring. I was below. I ran on deck just as we struck into another ship. She was a foreigner by their lingo. I ran forward to see if the boatswain and carpenter was all right, for they slept there. They were all right, so I got some hurricane lamps lit. Then me and the chief officer went to find how much we had been damaged. I got down the fore-peak ladder two rungs, when I found I was in water. You could have rowed two boats through the hole in her bow. We took hatches off the fore-hold. I made to go down again, when on the ladder's second rung I was in water. So that was 18 feet of water in the fore-hold.

Our ship was 28 years old and the skipper and chief engineer was afraid of the engine bulkhead, for there was only that one between the engine room and 18 feet of water and the fore-hold was a large hold. Owing to having a Greek seaman in my watch, I found it was a Greek steamer we had run into. He told us they cried out for us to save them, so we put our second officer and the Greek on board of her and tried to tow her back to Bembridge into shoal water. But we broke all our hawsers, so we gave it up. On the way into Bembridge we met a patrol ship and we made for shallow water as fast as we could. We anchored in four and a half fathoms, and then we thought we were pretty safe for a time, but at daylight after seeing the state we were in we made for Southampton Water off Netley. We anchored and the Company's Super came on board to say, 'No dock for you at Southampton. Go to Cardiff. There's a dock there for you.' Fancy what a trip with 18 feet of water in the fore-hold, a hole in the bow you could row two boats abreast through. Anyway we managed to get and dock at Cardiff. When owing to the strain I had had (the skipper would only trust me at the wheel; then he would relieve me to see to mooring of the ship) I had contracted a hernia. The shore doctor came on board and said I must not go to sea without a doctor being on board the ship and I ought to have an operation. Would I go in hospital at Cardiff? I said, 'No, I would not be operated on in Cardiff.' The doctor said he would try the strongest truss he could get. He got the strongest one he could get, tried it, but the next day he found it was no good, so he said I must be operated on. So the skipper came to me and said he would discharge me on board; and all he could do, as they had found it was an old complaint brought on through strain, was to give me the truss and pay my fare home, and I could rejoin the ship if I got well soon enough, as he had recommended me to the company and he did not wish to lose what you would call a sailor. If I came back to the company I was down for promotion as soon as any vacancy occurred. I was down for boatswain of the new ship the company was building and I would not stop at that rank.

They found out there was a nurse travelling to Southampton to join a hospital ship there, and they put me in her charge as I was in a bad state, but I managed to get home. The nurse was very good to me. I went in the Southampton and Hants Hospital and I had a bad time. They sent for my wife, I was that bad! But I managed to pull through and I could not rejoin my ship as the doctors said I ought to have very light work on shore for three or four years. So after about three months' rest, I got into the sail-making department at Thornycrofts, Woolston, and there I stayed having started.

At the beginning of 1918, after being in the loft for six months, a sit-down job, I asked to be allowed to go out on trial in the new torpedo boats as they were built. I think I went out in 16 of them but I happened to be working in the sail loft when the bells rang out for peace.

My dear wife left that morning by the 11 o'clock train for Newport, Monmouthshire, where our daughter Fanny was very ill. I followed her down on the Saturday. As there was no trams

Tom's daughter Fanny, who died in the flu epidemic of 1918,
with her husband Tom Brown.

running at Newport and the streets were so crowded, I got to my daughter's door just too late to see her alive. She died, and her two children in a week, with the bad attack of the 'flu in 1918. She died on the 18th of November, 1918. It was a good ending of the war, but a sad time for me and my wife.

So we said goodbye to the year 1918.

* * *

I worked for Thornycrofts till August, 1919, then we had ten days' holiday for stocktaking, so myself and five other riggers was asked by the shore boatswain to go and work on the 9-inch mooring-wires what they wanted made ready for the German mail boat *Imperator*[1], afterwards named *Berengaria*. On cutting up a couple of 9-inch towing-hawsers of 120 fathom in length, we made four mooring-wires and two of 8-inch; we made four more in the ten days. So we went back to Thornycrofts for three weeks. Then, as they was reducing hands, I went and started for the Cunard as shore boatswain. I continued working for the Cunard Company. I was mostly on the *Imperator*. It was about the time that ships what had belonged to the Germans before the war was suddenly addicted to the game of catching fire in our harbours and also in the American harbours as well. So I was signalled out to take charge of the fire-station on the *Imperator's* boat deck. I had 12 other sailors out of the shore gang to man the station. She had a good size one, but everything and all markings was in German and myself understanding the German language was the reason of being in charge. I knew that there was one faulty indicator which, if it became extra warm, fell on 'fire'. It was for B deck section and one warm night it fell. The man on watch called me at once, saying one of the indicators had fallen for fire, but it was the faulty one. I called the fire brigade and made them all dress up in their fire gear. Sending the watchman to call the ship's officer to notify that there were a fire on B Deck. I done it to train the men. They did not know that it was faulty, but by the time ship's officer joined us we had everything ready for the 'fire' on B deck. I took the officer with us to the supposed fire and when I got them there and everything, hose and all laid on ready for the fire, all but turning the water on, I told them it was a false alarm. The officer said, 'Did you time yourself?'

'Yes, sir – seven minutes and everything in working order.'

'Well, Diaper, you got a smart set of firemen. You done well and it was good training for the men in case we did have a fire. A tot of rum for all!'

The fire crew called me an artful codger, saying all I wanted was a tot of rum. Why not? But I am afraid it won't pass off another time, for the tot I mean, but only for a real fire.

By good luck and having so many detectives about the ship no one had the chance to set fire to the Imperator. When she was ready for sea the skipper wanted me to go as chief fireman, but I would not. I worked by the company, taking detective at times.

13
Trans-Atlantic in
Shamrock

now I could pick 35 men now
and only have one gentleman
to take the time and a yankee
to represent America, him to see
fair play and my self in command
I would sail Shamrock IV and ?
I tell you I would beat the
resolute.

For 1920 I had shipped in the *Shamrock*[1] 23-metre as second mate under my brother, Alf Diaper, who was the skipper of her. We started on the 15th February to make her ready to cross the Atlantic to act as trial-horse to train and tune up the *Shamrock* IV[2] which was already over there. She went over in 1914, only the war came on. The *Shamrock* 23-metre was not one of the *Shamrocks* built for the America's Cup, but built to race around the British coast regattas, so, as I said, we started to make ready.

The *Shamrock* 23-metre was over at Camper & Nicholson's yard. Jim Gilby, the mate, was getting her ready with the port watch for the crossing under her ocean rig. She was being made into yawl rig for the crossing, while I, the second mate, with the starboard watch, was cleaning and making and packing all her racing gear – sails, spars, and all the halyards, etc – and labelling it to go across in one of the Cunard boats; we had to take the weight of everything. Quite a big job it is to pack a 23-metre racing gear, but we managed to get it done by the 1st April, and the Shamrock was launched and towed out of the river. The compass was adjusted and we moored off Southampton on the Test. The next day, 2nd April, we went for a short sail with the owner on board. While I was steering her back to her moorings, he wished us luck and hoped I would keep a good log of the voyage across, as, after it was all over, he wanted the log book in London to read to his guest when he came to dinner, which had been arranged whether we won or lost. He hoped there would be something in the book to start a big laugh. So Sir Thomas Lipton and his guest, Lord Delaware, wishing us a good and quick voyage across the Atlantic, with 'God speed you' they went on shore.

The next day, 3rd April, all hands went on shore and signed on to take Shamrock 23-metre to America and bring her back to Southampton after the races for the America's Cup, whether they were won or lost, if required to do so. We left Southampton 5th April and let go anchor off Yarmouth, Isle of Wight, for the night to catch a fair ebb-tide through the Needles passage, for the wind was dead against us all the way down the English Channel. We left Yarmouth the morning of the 7th April, 1920, and sure enough had the wind ahead the whole way down to Falmouth, where we put in and anchored so that we might do some little alterations what wanted doing for the passage across. It was well for us we had done so, for that night it came on to blow a very hard gale, continuing for almost a fortnight. Then the gale fined down to a light wind. We left Falmouth and had got about 30 miles to the south-west of Land's End, when the gale came on with redoubled fury. So we ran back to Falmouth again. On the fourth day in there, we made another start, the wind still hanging in the west. We made the first leg of our journey to Ushant, when we put her on the other tack, standing off to make a good clearance of that dangerous point, the wind beginning to increase and the sea

TRANS-ATLANTIC IN *SHAMROCK*

getting up. We kept tacking her up to the windward till the third night out of Falmouth, no one getting any rest, it was so rough. On this third night out I went on watch at 12 o'clock midnight, I had just relieved them when an able-seaman asked me to take a look around the forecastle. I did, and quickly got the captain and navigator to look also. This is what I saw. An iron stanchion in the centre of the forecastle, which was a deck support, was starting to bend, which should not have been, but the pounding of her long bow and the heavy seas pounding her deck was causing that – and not only that. The fishplate what ran around each side of the ship, underneath the covering board, was half-inch steel plating and it was bending the port and starboard in line across the deck with the iron stanchion, all in a line bending together. Myself, having had more than anyone on board of sea-going, in that class of ship, warned them that if we kept on pounding her bow in such a storm much longer, the Shamrock would not reach America. Why not then turn back and wait for a better chance of luck and a fair wind? The skipper and navigator together said, 'We dare not turn back for Sir Thomas Lipton wants this boat in America.'

I myself answered, 'To h— with Sir Thomas! He looked out for himself not to be here with us. There are 22 of us on board, and 68 in England depending on us. What will they all do if we are lost? The owner cannot look after them, and you know the boats is no good to save us. Now will you listen to me this once, for I have had a lot of experience in this kind of craft. It is 12.20 and I will try to keep her going until 2am, and if it is no better by then I will turn her round and make for the first port we can reach in safety. The only way you will get this boat to America is by running away from it now in this storm. I will take the blame, if there is any.' So that was agreed on. They went below, being worn out by their long watch on deck in the gale. The strain had told on the skipper who was ill; it was physically impossible for him to carry on longer on deck. At 15 minutes before 2am, I called an able seaman, saying, 'Go below, see the first mate, tell him to get all hands out and make ready to turn the ship round.'

So when the first mate came on deck, he said, 'The skipper wants you, the weather is worse now, Tom.' I replied, 'At times it's a devil of a lot worse.' I went below.

The skipper said, 'What is it like on deck, Tom? It is hard enough below.' I said, 'It's that bad, skipper, that I have warned the watch to just rope themselves, for you have a hard job to see the big ones coming. Skipper, it will be risky job turning her in this hurricane.'

'Are you going to wear or gybe her, Tom?'

'No, neither. I am going to stay her' (or, in plain words, tack her round), 'and I am steering her.'

To the navigator, I said, 'After I get her round, I will see what is on the log and keep her north-east course till I report to you.'

The skipper gave me a tot of whisky; 'I don't want this to buck me up, only for good luck,' I said. Then I went on deck, saw the first mate. I said, 'Jim, I will take the wheel, for I am going to sail her until everything is ready for tacking.'

'Yes, Tom,' he answered.

'Now, you, Jim,' I said, 'go forward to the main rigging. Have a rope to put around you for safety and when I call out to you, you will be looking for a dark spot in the waves. Call out like hell, "A dark spot, Tom." Then I will, if I have enough way on and the ship answers all right, lee-ho, and every man for himself.'

So only a short space of time had gone by, and I had offered up a short prayer, for guidance and safety in the job I was going to do – the same as I had always done since I started going to sea, to the only One up above Who can see you safely through anything, good or danger, if you ask Him – when the mate's voice came, 'A dark spot coming, Tommy.'

'All right,' I answered, 'and every man for himself.'

Now every man was at his station and everything went just like clockwork. We got that ship round, in spite of the mountainous seas and a hurricane of wind and dark as a dungeon, as well as if we were on a mill-pond, without shipping a pail of water, or breaking a rope yarn. That was the time that Sir Thomas Lipton ought to have been with us, trying to cross the Atlantic. So having got her round, I set the course north-east, and went below to report to the navigator the course and distance on the log, and had put the oil bags over. Then, turning to the captain I said, 'I don't think a tot of whisky would hurt the men. It will act like medicine. I will enter it in the official log as such.'

'Well, Tom,' he said, 'I reckon you all deserve it; you all done a good job. I nearly thought I had got into the Solent.'

But I answered, 'It was a bit too jumpy to think that! But we had a lucky turning.' We drank our tot and then the watch below turned in, or lay down somewhere to try and get some rest. I returned to my watch on deck, but, owing to the wind veering more to the west and making the heavy seas coming more on the quarter, we could not make a true north-easterly course for Falmouth. The navigator was a bit worried, and the skipper too, but I said, 'We shall make Dartmouth, what's the odds? We can get repairs done there.' For when we did get there we looked a proper wreck on deck. The lashings had pulled the stem-pieces away from the two 18-foot lifeboats, all the plank ends had pulled away from the stems, and both boats had to be made seaworthy.

We stayed till the repairs were finished in about a week, repairing the mainsail which we had partly blown away, and then we made a fresh start from which we did not turn back.

We had a headwind when we started, and we fetched over to Ushant again, then put about on the other tack. When we were 80 miles by the log, the wind changed more to the north-west, so we went about and had a bit of free sheet and we carried that wind to the Azores in about seven days. There we replenished our stores and water-tanks, and started on the rest of the voyage, making the whole journey in two days, seven hours. Not bad, considering we had a two-day calm and paltry weather, just south of the Gulf Stream, about seven days out from the Azores. In fact, we and the crew was catching small crabs on the seaweed drifting out of the Gulf Stream. From the Azores to New York we had two separate moderate gales lasting 12 hours each with light variable winds in between. But the gales were with us, and they drove us about 12 knots – not bad, loaded down like we were, fully rigged.

* * *

We reached New York. At the entrance the Customs cleared us and we were towed to City Island, New York Yacht Yard, where the yard went to work to change the ocean gear into the racing gear, that had arrived out long before we got there. We were in them in a week, all but the topmast. We had to leave that on deck; with it up in place we was 175 feet from the deck to the top of the topmast, too tall to go under Brooklyn Bridge. We were soon ready to help tune up the Shamrock IV. We had some races together. She had three out of five against us, but she did not win the cup – too many amateur sailing masters. In fact I have before me now a photograph out of a New York newspaper with the Resolute[3] catching the Shamrock up quick, when it ought to be the other way about – the Shamrock leaving the Resolute behind. The Shamrock lost the cup where she ought to have won it. In fact, Sir Thomas Lipton and Lord Delaware came on our Shamrock on November 27th, and said he had done wrong to lose the cup. Our crew was the one that ought to have been on Shamrock IV. He would have taken any odds on it, but he found out too late.

Shamrock IV. © Beken of Cowes.

So they decided to lay *Shamrock* 23-metre up at City Island, and send both crews home.

It was while laying up – we were having a rest the Sunday before we were leaving for home (I was below, having a bath, etc) – that a deck able seaman called out, 'Mr Diaper, here is a gentleman who would like to see you,' so with that I went on deck. The gentleman then said, 'That is the one. I should know him in a crowd! Can you place me, Tom?'

For some time I looked at him, then I said, 'I cannot place you yet.'

So he replied, 'I will try to recall your memory. Do you remember in the village of Itchen, a public house called "The Yacht Tavern"; the landlord was Captain T Diaper, your father. He had been pilot of the American yacht *Navahoe*. I was talking to him when you came in. You shook hands with me, and asked me to have a drink and I had a glass of barley wine with you. I turned round to leave, and you said, "I will walk to the floating bridge with you." We had just got outside, when I suddenly spun round and would have fallen, if you had not caught hold of me, and you said, "That was that drink of barley wine that done that!"'

'Right,' I replied, 'you are the mate, Mr Jeffreys, late of the *Navahoe*. I place you now! How are you?'

'Fine, you are the kind of chap that I have been looking for,' he said. 'You see that large sailing yacht lying off in the bay, the one with three mast-yards on the fore-mast. Well, I am captain of that hooker; she is the largest sailing yacht in America. Now, the lay is this: we propose to come over to Southampton and have two motors put in her, and when ready, to cruise round the south coast of England, then over to the Baltic to cruise along the coast of Sweden, Norway, Denmark, Russia and Finland. I have heard a lot about you from Yankees what have been over there, and you know I shipped you for the *Virginia* II when I was captain of *Virginia* I. I propose, as soon as I arrive at Southampton, to ship you as my pilot for two pounds per day, seven days a week, and all found.

Sir Thomas Lipton with the crew of *Shamrock IV*. Thomas Lipton is in the centre, Tom's brother Alf to his right and on the same row third in from the left is Tom.

All I shall want you to do is to put me in a good anchorage. I will take her from place to place. Will you be agreeable to that, Tom?'

'Right,' says I, 'shake on it, and come below and have a drink on it. No, not barley this time, but a good drop of Scotch "White Horse."' So we parted the best of friends, and I have not seen him since, as you will hear later. Now the day after that, I was sent for by Lipton's manager, to go to him on the house-boat. When I arrived there all the officers of both *Shamrocks* were assembled there. The first words I heard from the manager were, 'Where is your brother, the skipper of the *Shamrock*?' I replied, 'You ought to know where he is, for you know "I am not my brother's keeper."' 'Well,' he said, 'you are the one that has taken the three inventories; first: the one suit of racing gear, second: the ocean-going rig, third: all the spare sails and gear not to go. But what I want to know is, where is the round piece of wood which goes on the end of the main boom with the shamrock leaves carved on it?' I replied, 'Well, sir, here are the three inventories complete. If you can find it on the inventory, it is in the store with the rest of the gear. For all that is in the stores, I am the one that is responsible, and I will stand by my responsibility.'

'Well,' he said later, 'it is not on the lists. Where is it? I must know, for I have got to send it to Sir Thomas in London, with Shamrock IV's wheel and compass. Now come on, where is it?'

'Well,' I replied, 'the last time I saw it was on the ship in its place on the boom end, and I don't remember seeing it since then. Now, remember, one wants the eyes of a hawk to watch these G—damn Yanks, or they would steal the teeth out of your head to sell for souvenirs of the Shamrock at the present time.' The manager then said, 'I hold you responsible for it, Diaper, and if it is not forthcoming I will have your bag and luggage searched on arrival at Southampton.'

'Well – you say that now, and I say this now, and mean it. If by any chance I catch anyone outside the Customs' men laying their hands on my luggage, be it you, or anyone told by you to do it, I will try to give him the biggest tanning he's had in his life. That comes from an honest man's mouth.'

The skipper of the Shamrock IV touched my arm and said, 'Keep quiet, mate. You will be getting into trouble.' The manager said to the skipper, 'You keep quiet, skipper. I should still like to know why, when asked to race on board the Shamrock IV, Tom Diaper did not do so.'

'Well, I can tell you, that when my brother had raced on her three times, it was on the third race that he said he had sprained his wrist. He said you told him that I had to go on the fourth day, but I said to my brother, "You can say I am a racing man, and that sooner than race with the likes of them that is trying to sail the Shamrock IV, sooner than be seen racing aboard with them in command, I would go back to England." And this is what I say – I could pick 35 men now, and have only one gentleman to take the time, and a Yankee to represent America, and to see fair play, with myself in command. I would sail *Shamrock IV*, and I tell you I would beat the *Resolute!*'

That caused it all right. 'Diaper, I've finished with you.'

'Thank you,' said I, 'but don't forget the lost shamrock, and the luggage search – and what would happen after I got back on board!' Our first mate said, 'Well, Tom, you have caused them on *Shamrock IV* to look down their noses a bit, and to tell you the straight tip, Tom, I know that you could do it, as I have seen you do it when you was skipper in Germany – I was one of the crew of a boat racing against you. It is as I said before, Tom, you were a top man at the game in Germany, and when they finished having Englishmen, you come back and try to get a job in the same position again; it is like you had to start your life all over again.'

'Well, Jim, I am not in the circle, a percentage-man.'

'What do you mean by that, Tom?'

'I will let you into the secret when we are alone, Jim.'

So, two days after that, both crews went on board of the *Lapland*[4]; it was a Belgian ship, but under the Yankee flag and crew, with second-class passengers. The second day out, the chief officer came up and said, 'Your crew tells me that you are the Diaper of the *Shamrock*. I should like to shake hands with you, I am that pleased to have you on board. Come with me, I will introduce you to the captain.' The captain shook hands and asked if I was satisfied with my cabin and cabin-mate. Well my mate was a Chinaman, so I replied, 'My cabin's all right, but I rather object to having a "Chink" for a cabin-mate.' The captain said, 'Take him to the purser, chief.' So to the purser I went. His words was, 'Do you like it in your first cup of coffee, or will you come to my cabin and have it there as soon as you get up?' So it was arranged this way. The purser, a little later, took me to a first-class cabin and put a stewardess to look after me. He asked me if I liked fruit. 'Yes,' I replied, 'and so does my crew.' 'All right,' he answered, 'I will have a case put in your cabin, so you can give the crew some, for you should know what sailors are.'

Well, it was a lovely trip over 'the Herring Pond', as the Yanks call it, smooth and calm, fine weather all the way. On arriving at Southampton, we were supposed to go straight to the Shipping Office to be paid off, but there was a runner there. He put us all in cabs, and then paid the fare to our homes. After being home a week and getting no money, the crew came to me to know what to do about it. Well, they would not listen to me. They was going to write. They did.

The pay was held up, because the skipper, having stayed as detective for the Cunard on the quayside at New York, had forgotten to send the wage pay book. Owing to not taking my advice, the crew only got paid up to the time of landing at Southampton. But I got paid for three weeks after landing, by only writing a civil letter that I expected to be paid up to the time they received the wage book.

So that ends a bit of adventure going to America to see an English yacht bring the cup away, but they will never do it the way they try too many captains. All that is needed to race a yacht, is one captain, with one crew, one timekeeper, and one pilot. Two or three guests, but no one to interfere with the captain – without he is going to hit another boat, that should be pointed out.

* * *

After getting back from the *Shamrock* and America, I worked for the shore boatswain of the Cunard Line at Southampton Docks up till January, 1921, when I expected Captain Jeffreys to arrive with the American yacht which I was going to be pilot of; but in the meantime the great strike of the joiners came on, and all work on the inside of vessels were cancelled. So the Americans having heard of the strike, I received a letter to the effect that the cruise to the Baltic was cancelled and they were going to the South Sea Islands instead, so that put paid to my pilot's job. I continued to work on till the end of March, when I shipped as skipper in a 22-ton pleasure yacht, the *Patience*[5]. I stayed in her till the end of September, 1921. A funny thing that happened was that the manager of the *Shamrock* was brother to the owner of the yacht *Patience* I was skipper of, and he had a week's holiday on board of us. He promised that when the *Shamrock* came back from America I should be her captain. He gave me a two-pound tip for looking after him. When I saw him as soon as the *Shamrock* arrived in England and I asked him about the skipper job, he said, 'That is all there is in it for you.' So that put paid to that year of 1921.

So I had to fall back into the sail loft of the Cunard Company, where I served again and acted as special detective at times when they required it, up till the end of May, 1922. So on the 1st June I shipped with a Mr Brereton on his yacht *Kate*[6], a sailing yacht of 20 tons. We cruised along the south coast of England. At Dartmouth the headmaster and his assistants came on board from the Royal Naval College, Dartmouth, for naval cadets. We cruised down to Land's End, calling at all places. Although they were headmasters at the game, in a gale of wind what caught us off Start Point, I showed them a bit of seamanship what they had never seen before, of shifting sails, and a ship in a gale of wind without doing damage to anything.

* * *

Now came 1923; I could not get a skipper's job this year so I shipped as second mate on board the large racing yacht *Terpsichore*[7].

It was in this yacht that I could have done myself a bit of good, and would have brought myself to the notice of the yacht-racing world again, but I refused to jump over another man's head to take charge of the yacht. It was while the other man was on board the same ship when I was asked to do that, at Cowes Regattas, but I told them: 'When the yacht is laid up, and all hands paid off, send for me then and I would take charge.' So we went into White's to pay off. The owner, Mr R H Lee, took my address and was going to send for me to take charge of *Terpsichore* on the 1st January, 1924, and I am confident I should have made myself for life, but before the time came for me to do that, and before we had finished laying up, the sad news came that the owner had passed away while out shooting. He had a stroke and in less than two hours had passed away. So we were all paid off.

14
Pinkerton Detective Agency

*That is how I meet The Pinkerton
of The Pinkerton Detective agency.
Now Skipper you have done Exceedingly
well I think you have the making
of a good Detective with me. I use
Yachting has a screen to my usual
Employment*

Now in January of 1924 I was sent for by Mr Kemp of Hythe Yacht Yard. When I got there he told me that a Mr Pinkerton had asked him to find a skipper for his yacht, a 60-ton sailing yawl, *Mollihawk*[1], what he had bought from a French gentleman, and if he found a skipper, would he be ready to take charge from the French crew (what was bringing her over from France), and check over the inventory and to see that everything in general was OK. Well, I accepted the job and the next day I had a 'phone message to say she had arrived, and would I come over at once, as the French skipper would not allow anyone on board, 'only Diaper, the skipper.' Well, I got over all the speed I could muster, and if ever I saw a madman, that French skipper was like one. What with a mixture of French and broken English, I made out from him that they had a terrible storm coming over. He said they tried to anchor in mid-Channel. As we started to take the inventory on deck, he told me he had lost the port anchor and

30 fathoms of chain. I stopped at that and went on shore, saying I had to get a gentleman on board, then I would take her over. As she was insured under Lloyds, I got Kemp to 'phone for a Lloyds' agent to come over to go on board with me. He came and you should have seen the yawl when we went below.

She had been a beautifully fitted yacht below, but now it was a complete wreck, just as though someone had been knocking all the furniture to pieces with a big sledge-hammer. She was also half full of water. We asked him how the water had got in. He said, 'Through the covering-board seam.' After we had inspected everywhere, we saw the covering-board seam. The putty stopping was not even cracked. I was of the opinion that one of them had used one of the lavatories, and had forgotten to turn the inlet tap off till the water had got 1 foot above the seat of the lavatory. Then they must have put her so that she listed well down, for we found coke right up to her deck, under the lining. That is how I explained to the agent, but we made the skipper write and put everything what had happened in the ship's log, and let them go while I took charge. I am sure to this day that was what happened, both from inquiring of a skipper who I knew was in the Channel that night, and because her deck showed no signs of hard weather. That is how, with the yawl under the insurance agents and Lloyds' underwriters, I got a crew for the yawl Mollihawk, which Pinkerton owned and had almost fitted her out when I had to get her out of Hythe Lake and moor her off afloat and I was not to let a soul know that Pinkerton would come on board when it was dark and give me instructions what I was to do. He came at 10pm. That is how I met The Pinkerton of the Pinkerton Detective Agency.

'Now, skipper, you have done exceedingly well. I think you have the making of a good detective with me. I use yachting as a screen to my usual employment. Now this is for tomorrow.

The Prince of Wales is coming down to Southampton to open the new floating dock[2] the day after tomorrow and tomorrow I want you to take the launch and take your family as though you was on pleasure. Land them at whatever landing places you know of which has access to Southampton and the Docks. You must display a certain flag. Here it is on a staff on the bow of the launch and everywhere you land there will be a man of mine placed there. As soon as you have left that place and every place you have landed at, so every place will be guarded by the time the Prince arrives.' Well, I done that by the early evening, it being a fine day. The wife and kiddies said they had enjoyed themselves and what a fine man my boss must be.

The next day came and everything afloat was decorated with flags, but not us. About 9am Pinkerton just peeped up the hatch to look on deck. 'What, skipper, no decorating?' he said.

'Awaiting your orders,' I replied. 'Quite right. Only about four flags up the foremast and that flag you had on the launch at the top. There will only be one man in Southampton who knows I am in this place. I am the unknown detective who for safety's sake has to look after the Prince. We are supposed to be having trials. As soon as the boat comes out of the dock you will know which one he is on board, for as soon as they see the boat (the Mollihawk) with that flag on top they will hoist one the same as that and you are to place yourself with the yacht and head the way down the river, a piece turn and head him right up to the tape he is to break; but if danger should arise and you have the order to break that tape before the Prince's ship arrives to it, could you break the tape and bring this yacht out of the dock?' I said, 'Yes I could.'

Now the Mollihawk had port holes all around her, so Pinkerton could see what was going on. So I planted ourselves about 50 yards ahead. I thought I should have to take the danger first or stop it if that danger should arise. 'Well,' says I, 'here is the chap to do his best if the case should arise.' On the way to the floating dock they had police boats out to keep the way clear. They came to make us get off the course to the dock, when a loud voice called out, 'Let that yacht proceed on her way. Don't stop her.' I tell you my fingers was beginning to twing. We was getting near the tape, we were almost on top of it when the cry rang out: 'All clear. Sheer off! Don't break it!' Good job I had a quick-moving boat or I should not have done it. But Pinkerton was pleased and we celebrated when we got to our moorings and Captain Steel of the White Star Line, who was friendly with Pinkerton, congratulated me when we had the story all over again on the way I handled the Mollihawk. 'The right man and the right boat could not have done better, skipper,' he said.

Now that the opening of the floating dock by the Prince was finished, myself and the crew settled down on the work of making the Mollihawk look what she really was – a first-class yacht. But in between whiles I done a few short detective stunts for Pinkerton to his satisfaction. I took Mollihawk over to St Malo or opposite to Dinard really, for a Frenchman had chartered her for one month. We fished all around the Channel Islands for the first two weeks, when the charterer came to me and asked if it was possible for me to get in touch with Pinkerton to see if he would extend the charter for a month longer, making on the whole two months. I did and I got the extension. Had I known at the time what I had to go through day and night, I would have asked the owner to have finished the charter at the month. Only you can't always know what you have got to go through, especially down at Biarritz, where we lay in the nearest harbour 5 miles from it, for Biarritz has no harbour, only all rocks in front of the main hotel where the party was to stay. Then to motor round to Jean de Luce, a place as I say is 5 miles from Biarritz. We were the only boat that lay in the outer harbour the whole month. There is only a breakwater there, but they cannot keep it whole for as fast as they repair it a gale of wind comes and the heavy seas wash the east end away. We was in the Bay of Biscay five weeks and we was never laying still all that time. Whether we was sailing or at anchor it was roll, roll, all the time.

Well, all things have an ending and that charter came to an end and so we made all the speed we could to get to the River Itchen and moored in White's Yard for a week to rest our sore ribs. Although I had had orders to go to Lymington from Pinkerton, he told me afterwards that he was on the look for us to pass Totland Bay, but it was too dark a morning for him to see us. So after that we cruised about inside the Isle of Wight, then laid her up for the winter at Hythe Yacht Yard. They had hauled the big yawl up there, so the *Mollihawk* crew was paid off and I made my change over to look after the owner's interest in the yawl. I slept on board of her that winter of 1924–1925 for the yard was taking the lead keel off and sawing it into pieces. I had to see to the weighing and the selling of it, for at that time the lead was a high price and the owner was making his money out of it.

* * *

In the spring of 1925 we fitted out *Mollihawk* to live on board and cruise about the Solent, laying at anchor most of the time, off White's, for the doctors had told Pinkerton that the smell of that mud was good for his complaint, for he was always pasty-looking without he was on a special job.

After the yawl had all her lead taken away and sold, she herself was sold by auction and all her gear was put up and sold the same way, but it all came back to the owner. The yawl was launched off from Hythe and taken over to the yard at Lloyd's next to Thornycroft's who had the job to replace the lead keel with an iron one and put iron ballast inside.

So after laying Mollihawk up at Sheppard's Yard on the Hamble River, I returned to my home at Itchen, going daily to the yard, getting all her rigging together to fit out.

In 1926 when March came, I shipped a crew for the yawl and we fitted her out. Thornycroft's had put two motors in her, placed between the saloon which had been shortened in length, and the forecastle which had been shortened also.

So we cruised about a bit to get everything ship-shape. The owner let her on charter for six weeks. That is the worst of having charge of a charter. The character tries all he can to get 25 hours out of 24 hours a day, but I will say we was at it 23 hours a day all that six weeks.

With the finish of 1926 season we put all sail gear away and moored to buoys on the River Hamble and used her for the winter of 1926–1927 for a house-boat. Then in April, 1927, fitted her out for to do some cruising about.

The owner asked me would I lay the yawl at Lloyd's Yard, Woolston, and keep an eye on Mollihawk on the Hamble? Well, we had laid the yawl up, paid all hands off, myself and all.

I went to work at Harland & Wolff with the shore boatswain when I had a wire to go to the Mollihawk and give her a good go over. I put in two weekends and was still working for Harlands when my wife brought me a wire from Pinkerton asking me to meet him at the bottom of the High Street, Southampton.

I met him. He was in a hurry to catch a tram to the train to Chislehurst, Kent, then back to America.

'How would a £25 cheque do you?' He got in the tram, called 'Goodbye,' and that was that!

* * *

It was still late summer of 1927. I went to work after Pinkerton had gone. The next day found that my gang had worked all through the night, so we finished work at 5 o'clock and lo and behold, when I got home my wife says, 'There is a letter for you, Dad, I have not opened it.' Well I did and inside was a £25 cheque, the letter saying, 'A present for you, skipper,' for it was through me having the Mollihawk so clean and perfect he had sold it and if I could sell the yawl's trysail to the same man I could have one-third of what I got for it. Would I show it to them the next Saturday?

I did and before the next week was over I had a letter from Pinkerton thanking me, wishing me goodbye, with a ten-pound cheque inside, saying he had received 30 pounds for the trysail and was very pleased with what I had done, and the ten pounds was the third of the 30 pounds!

* * *

It was in September, 1927, when I was sent for to go to Lloyd's Yacht Yard, Woolston, to see a gentleman. When I saw him, he asked me if I was prepared to go up to Hammersmith and fetch a large motor launch from there down, and put her alongside the house-boat Florinda[3]. The launch was called Florinda II[4].

So I went and brought her down and placed her as required. Then he shipped me as skipper of his house-boat and all he had afloat.

I stayed in that job till September, 1928. Then we had a disagreement and I finished up with that job. I did not like it all the time I was in it, as he shifted the house-boat to Poole Harbour, bought a fishing boat and wanted me to take the men out fishing night time, as well as day. That made me finish.

So that put paid to 1928 yachting, if you could call it that. So for the winter of 1928–1929 I went and worked for Risdon Beazley at Northam Bridge.

* * *

In March, 1929, I took a large motor launch for him from his yard and handed her over to the owner at the Cattewater, Plymouth. On my return I took charge of a large steam hopper what he had bought and we dredged White's Lake out. We filled our dredger first and then I took her out off the Nab Light Tower, emptied her, then proceeded up to the Thames and picked up a towing hopper. We brought her back to White's Yard and then filled her (as well as ourselves) day-time and towed her with us out to the dumping ground in the Channel, night-time, getting back to White's Lake by day-light, so that we could start to re-fill them again. We carried that on for about 12 days and had about one more day's work to finish the lake, when the boss sent for me to take the 40-foot Thornycroft twin-motor launch up to Southend to try in the motor race from there to Cowes. We had two motor-men of our own from our yard and one from Thornycroft's. I had another rigger to help me on deck and we was to start the race at Southend at 12 noon. We filled up with petrol and started with about 20 others. We was the first to reach Cowes, the time being 2am Sunday morning, the second motor yacht arriving at 6am. We had won the prize by the speed trial and stability. But through not having a recognized club member on board we lost the prize through that.

Towards the end of August I was sent down to Poole Harbour to do a job on a trawler converted into a yacht. An east-country skipper moored her up with rotten ropes. They had broken on the ebb tide in the night and he said if the owner took a fancy to me he might ask me to take him for a cruise down westward. Well, we was two days fixing her up, then the owner asked me to take him down the west as far as Land's End. So I agreed, and I had a lovely time up to when we got back. They were nice people. When we started to lay up I had agreed with the owner to stay on with him all the year round. It would have just suited me but it was to be a let-down for me, for I had just got everything put away for the winter and the yacht was hauled up under cover, when the owner, came to me and said he had bad news to tell me. He says, 'I am sorry, skipper, but I have lost all my money in the Hatry Crash[5] and I am very sorry for myself and for you. I am broke. I shall have to part with you, for I cannot keep you on. I am finished for yachting, but Mr Beazley has promised to keep you employed at the yard for the time being.'

15
A Permanent Job at Last

The wind was blowing. Then that hard that you had to hold on to something solid when you was on the forecastle and we turned in for the night thankful that we was in a good harbour.

I stayed on at the yard up till March, 1930. I got fed up with working about on shore, so I finished with Beazley and took to myself and visited all the yacht yards. A week before Easter I went to White's Yard. I was having a look around when the engineer skipper of the *Aerolite*[1] came and asked me if I wanted a job. I said that was what I was looking for; so he said he required a man to take charge of the deck and to take her about and if I had my testimonies on me, would I go on board with him?

The owner being away, a Mr Gray would see me as he was on board at the time. So I went on board and Mr Gray gave me the job. The *Aerolite* was owned by Squadron-Commander Bird of the Supermarine, Itchen. I started on Easter Tuesday to fit her out. She had been a tug, but at the time she had two Kelvin motors put in her, after she had her steam engine taken out; and when I started they were cutting the boiler to pieces and taking that out of her and they made a double-bunk cabin of the engine-room. Any way we was already finished fitting out by the time the joiners had finished and Mr Gray asked me to take her to her mooring off Hythe and the owner Commander Bird would join her there.

Well he arrived about 2.30am Sunday, and told us we could have a 'lay-in,' for the man himself would not want anything done to the ship until after 1 o'clock luncheon. Then we went over to Cowes.

Well we cruised about the Solent and Spithead fishing and returned to Hythe in the morning. We done that up to the time of the Cowes August Regatta where we laid all the week full up with his guests. Then he asked me if I could take the yacht to Dartmouth. I replied I could do it. Then he told the engineer-skipper to have everything ready to leave when I thought it was advisable to leave for Dartmouth.

Well, we landed the owner at Hythe. After he was gone we all went home being Saturday, and the cook said he would keep the watch, so the rest of us had the weekend home.

So we all returned on board on Monday. The engineer asked me to his cabin, where he told me he did not like the way the owner kept asking me about taking the ship to Dartmouth. He ought to have asked him if he could take her as he was the captain in charge. I kept my peace for I did not like making a row. I only said, 'I shipped here as navigator to take this boat about and he is an understanding man. He knew it was me that was navigator. I was the man he should ask.' I said then, 'I want the stores and everything on board by Thursday noon for I want to leave at 3pm for Yarmouth, Isle of Wight, so as to leave there on Friday at 5am to carry the last of the ebb tide through the Needles passage and I hope, weather permitting, to be in Dartmouth and moored up by sunset.'

Well, we left Hythe at 3pm Thursday, stopped at Yarmouth for the night. Under way 5.30am, had a fine run till just before we reached Berry Head. The engineer wanted to put into Brixham for the night, but I would not then, for the weather threatened to change, the barometer falling fast. One engine conked out. The engineer said we should never reach Dartmouth. I told him to get the motor started again. Then I told his second man to see if he could start her. I asked them to hurry for the sea was getting rough and it was blowing harder and looking very bad. He got the motor running. We rounded the Point with about a mile and half to the entrance of Dartmouth, putting the sea on our broadside, and if ever you wanted to see a boat roll, you should have seen the *Aerolite*. That evening it was good job we had the boats in on deck, or I think she would have turned turtle. She rolled that heavy. We passed a converted trawler. She was coming out of Dartmouth. The words I said was, 'If I was in charge of that boat I would turn her round and anchor in Dartmouth again'; but she did not, I am sorry to say.

Well, we got in and there was no one more pleased than I was when I ran her up above the Second Ferry and moored her with the bower anchor. The wind was blowing then that hard that you had to hold on to something solid when you was on the forecastle and we turned in for the night, thankful that we was in a good harbour. The next day late in the afternoon someone rowed alongside who knew the engineer and asked me if I saw the trawler going out as we came in. I replied yes, and the words I said was this, 'If I was in charge of that boat I would turn her round back into Dartmouth for the night.' The man answered saying, 'It was a pity he did not hear you, so he might have taken your advice; but he cannot now, poor fellow, for that boat and all hands was lost a little farther down the coast.'

Well I think I will finish here for a time, for it makes you think when you recall anything bad like that. Goodnight.

* * *

We turned out next morning and started to give the boat a good clean up after making the passage. We had three days to make her look fit for the owner to come aboard again. We had news on the Wednesday morning to say he would arrive about 7pm and have dinner on board for eight people.

Well, they arrived about 8pm.

When we turned out the next morning it was nice and fine, and after the owner had looked all over the ship, he gave me praise for the ship and asked me if it was ready to take them to see the regatta at Tor Bay, as the yachts was all racing. So we got out of Dartmouth and they had a good view of the yachts racing. It was while we were cruising round that Commander Bird got asking me why I was not in a racing yacht, as I seemed to know what the yacht that was racing would do before they did it. I told him and he said to me, 'Would you take charge of this yacht now?' I told him I would not take charge as I had made a vow that I would not jump over another man's head while we were both on board the same yacht. I had my testimonies on board if he would care to read them; and when he laid the yacht up and had paid all hands off, if he cared to send for me then to take charge of the yacht and we came to terms, I would be willing to do what he asked me.

'Well,' says he, 'it is clear of traffic now. You get your testimonies. I will read them when we get to Dartmouth, but I can tell you now before that you has proved yourself efficient enough for me to take charge of my yacht.'

Well we anchored in Dartmouth each day and each night going out to see the racing. He gave me back my testimonies saying, 'Do take charge of this ship. Your testimony proved more than what I thought of you. I only wish you would take charge now. I want to see if you could find a small racing yacht for sale, for I would buy her for you to learn me the way to go racing. I dearly wish I had known of you years ago for you suits me in all ways. This yacht has seemed different since you has been on board.'

I told him of the West Solent Restricted Class. There was one called the *Harkaway*[2] what some Americans had been using for cruising about. I heard they were going back to the USA and I thought they wanted to sell her. 'Well,' he said, 'you take the yacht back to her mooring off Hythe and let me know when you are ready for me to come on board. I will come there and have one more week cruising about inside the Isle of Wight.' He left us the next morning and we left with the yacht the morning after and had a fine run up to the Needles, arriving there at sunset. Meeting a strong head ebb tide off Yarmouth, we let go anchor, for it was doubtful if there might be another yacht had possession of our mooring. If so it would have been awkward for us in the dark. Had a quiet night and at 8am in the morning 'phoned the Power Company, Hythe, to ask if any yacht was on our mooring, would they be kind enough to get off them, as we should arrive about 2pm and would require them. So we got

Harkaway leading the West Solent Class. © Beken of Cowes.

under way, reaching Hythe about 2.15pm, moored and squared up for the day, watch ashore going home with orders to be on board at 9am next morning.

We made the yacht ready in two days. The Commander came on board and cruised around Seaview, Cowes, Yarmouth and Lymington for one week and returned to Hythe where the owner asked me to take full charge. I gave him the same answer, 'No, not till everyone was paid off.' He left us for good, telling us to take her to White's Yard and lay her up for the winter. We went the next day to the yard and in two weeks had her laid up and finished. The engineer, still being the captain, paid us all off, me included, so that put finish for us that summer 1930.

16
Training a Female Crew

*Then his wife spoke Tom,
she said I expect you used to
say a lot and Bless us under
your breath when we crew on
Harkaway Done wrong and lost
you a first prize Well Madam
Says I you would be greatly
Shocked if you could hear it
Some Times but that is all in the Work*

1930 It was on the Saturday morning, three weeks after paying off
from *Aerolite*, I said to the wife, 'No good going anywhere today,
I will have a lay in.' There was a double knock at the door, my wife
said, 'That is the postman, Dad. I believe that is good news for you.'

I got up and sure enough it was for me from Mr Gray saying
that Commander James Bird would like for me to catch a train
from Southampton West Station at 10am Sunday morning to
Brockenhurst, get out there and he would be waiting for me in
his car, expenses enclosed. Well, I went as asked to do. Arriving at
Brockenhurst I saw the boss in the car. On getting close to him he
said, 'You made it then, Tom. Jump in and sit down. I am taking
you to Lymington to show you something.'

I said, 'I guess I know what it is.'

'Well,' he says, 'what?'

I replied, '*Harkaway.*'

'Correct,' he said. 'Now I must hurry. I am expecting a wire by
the time I get to Lymington.'

144

So away we went. Arriving at the yacht yard, he got his wire and coming to me he said, 'Tom, we must hurry over our business. I have to be in London as soon as possible. Can you get home from here.'

'Yes, sir, I can.'

So he took me to Mr Parker, the yard foreman-shipwright.

'This is my captain, Mr Parker,' says the boss. 'Do everything he wants to have done to *Harkaway*.'

'All right,' says Parker. 'If I do everything Captain Diaper wants done, I shall not do anything wrong. We were neighbours for years and you could not have a better man.'

'You are telling me,' the boss said. 'Tom, I leave you in charge now. I must away to London. I will tell Mr Gray to send you four weeks' wages instead of three for your inconvenience and you will be in White's Yard at 10 o'clock Tuesday. Just let me see you as I enter the yard, then I shall know where to find you when I leave it. Goodbye for the present till Tuesday.'

So I stayed with Parker. We arranged all the alterations to be done on *Harkaway* and an estimate and cost of alterations to be sent to me, so that I could confer with the boss. If it suited myself and him and if the cost met with our joint approval they were to start on the work at once. So I left the yard, had lunch and caught the 3pm bus and arrived home at 4pm, myself and wife well satisfied at the way things had turned out for us both that day.

Well I was in White's Yard on the Tuesday and saw the boss who acknowledged my salute to let me know he had seen me. So I waited about for about an hour when the boss came to me and told me he had given the engineer-skipper his notice, saying he made it clear to him that he must be away from the *Aerolite* by the next Friday, and put the keys of the yacht and store in the yard's office and the new skipper who was taking charge would collect them on the the following Monday.

'And that is you, Tom. Mr Gray will send you your wages as skipper, Tom, every Friday. You, Tom, will keep away from the yard this week. Have a holiday on pay and get the keys from the office next Monday and I think we shall have a pleasant time on *Aerolite* and *Harkaway* next summer with you in charge and learning me to go racing. So I wish you goodbye for the present. I am going abroad for the winter. Anything in what you want my advice about, just see Mr Gray and he will pass my word on to you.'

So I wished him bon voyage and said I would have both yachts ready for him the next summer, as soon as he let me know the date he wanted them for. So we parted at that, the end of October, 1930. It put my mind at rest to know I had a constant job and would not have to go searching for work week in week out and knowing I should be with my wife all the winter, as her health was failing and her eyesight was getting worse all the time. So I thanked God for the way the summer had proved for me and a promise of a Christmas dinner. The boss said I could rely on the biggest turkey he could get for myself and family to have a good Christmas dinner, and he kept his word.

* * *

I pottered about on the shore, doing rigging work where it was required and doing all kinds of jobs and going to the *Harkaway* at Lymington once a month. So 1930 passed away and 1931 came along. At the end of March news came that I could ship up a crew and have both yachts ready by the middle of May or thereabouts. So I done as requested; the boss came on board the 15th of May, where I had the *Aerolite* ready spick-and-span for him. He gave me praise for the way the yacht looked on deck and below. He had three days off Hythe, then we went to our mooring at Lymington what I had Parker to lay down for us

and I surprised him by the way I manoeuvred her in the narrow
waters and moored the ship up and the speed, the way it was
done. On the next day the boss and I went to the yard and had
Harkaway put in the water and towed down the river and put on
mooring close to *Aerolite*. We had our racing crew come on board.
The whole crew was the boss, his wife and two young ladies. All
except myself had never been on a racing yacht before, let alone
to go racing against the crews of the other boats of our class,
numbering about 20 of them, having the same crews what had
been on them for years. So I began by laying on the mooring,
hoisting the sail up and down and showing the way the ropes
should be made fast and the rope sheets should be made fast and
put on and off. Then the boss's wife said she had learnt enough
of that, she wanted to go sailing.

The boss winked at me, and said, 'What do you say, Tom? You
are the skipper. I have had enough of *Harkaway* for one day and I
expect you have too. Give your orders.'

'Well, all right. Stow the mainsail and coat him. Make up the
headsails, put them in their bags, haul all rope as tight as I showed
you. When you have finished that, get the dinghy alongside and
row me, the boss and yourselves to the *Aerolite* and we will finish
for the day. We will sail tomorrow if you behave yourselves.'

The boss's wife said, 'Why not go for a sail now?'

The boss said, 'Skipper has ordered to pack and tie up finished
for the day. You must obey him, so that is that. I could do with a
drink; what say you, skipper?'

'Every time, sir,' says I. So we went on board *Aerolite*, had our
drink and took it easy for the rest of the day.

The next day after sending the launch for the mail and fresh
provisions and cleaning *Aerolite* down, we went on board *Harkaway*
and our scratch crew made all ready to sail. The boss taking the
helm, we set sail and sailed out of the river. Then the starting boat

of the summer racing being in position, I made an imaginary course up round the West Solent Middle buoy, over to Yarmouth, round a yacht at anchor, back to starting point twice round. So explaining how we should start to the boss, I took the stop watch and checked the five minutes between the starting guns, instructing the boss what to do if we had another boat against us. It was a run to the West Middle and a beat to windward to Yarmouth. We set the spinnaker for the run to West Middle, not doing so bad with the female crew. We went round the course twice not doing so bad. The crew was tied in knots with the sheets. When we finished and had tied up on the mooring, the boss's wife said, 'I think, Tom, we crew knows everything there is to know about racing a yacht, don't you?'

I replied, 'If you do, I don't. I have been at it for 50 years, racing in all its phases and now I don't know it all and I have made a study of it all my life.'

The boss said, 'Tom, there is a race of our class here tomorrow. I won't race for a long time yet. Will you bring us out so that we may follow the class around?'

'A good idea, sir,' says I, 'then the crew will see if they has learnt it all or even a part of it. We will make her ready for racing. You say you has entered her in all races.'

So the next morning I told the boss to tell them they would have to show how smart they could be before so many yachts, for we did not want to look like a lot of landlubbers trying to imitate yachtsmen. There were 19 West Solent boats started all with spinnakers set at the start for the run up to West Middle. They were all on an even footing. We followed them over the line two minutes late. We did not set a spinnaker, running only under the set mainsail. The wind veered a bit to the west; all 19 boats had spinnakers set on starboard side, so the wind veering to the west caused the 19 boats to run by the lee and each one should gybe his sails over. But they were waiting for one another to start doing it, but no one did so. They ran all the way like that up to the West Middle. Well we were on the same gybe and we were running faster than them. I even had to pull our mainsheet in to stop us racing past them. We were the farthest away from the buoy, when I said, 'Shall I show our crew how I could get round the buoy?'

He said, 'If you like, Tom; the crew said you could not do it; you are farther away than any of them.'

'Now crew,' I says, 'we are in the race; pull in mainsheet and gybe her.' I half-turned the boat. When the others were 150 yards to go to the buoy, I half-turned on a reach with a 5-knot fair tide before they got their spinnakers in and gybed over. I was nearest the buoy and when we was level with the buoy I was first boat around it, head boat of the 20. So I says to the missus, 'That is another thing to learn.' Then suddenly the other boats began to creep up on us. One passed us, then I discovered the fault of that. The missus said she would make the main-sheet fast and this is what she had done. She had not fastened it properly. It was slipping very, very slowly, but it was enough, with the boss keep taking his attention off his steering and looking astern at other boats. He had better give up. When we got back to the starting point there were seven ahead of us. So we sailed to our moorings, stowed up, sat down and had a good conference, me explaining that I had got the lead, but could not keep it, as the crew did not know enough to keep on racing. So when racing they should pay special attention that when they had learnt the way to do a thing right, they should keep their wits and pay all their mind on their own work. I would watch the other boats and tell them when they could look at the other boats.

So we only raced a few times that year. We kind of played about, getting them used to all ways of sailing, but the boss improved greatly in the handling of the boat. Of course it was all amateur helmsmen in the small classes. We laid up at White's that year, laying *Harkaway* at Lymington, paid all hands off, but the engineer and one AB. Had *Aerolite* hauled up for the winter. We scaled her all over outside and under the waterline. The boss called me over to 11 London Road office and made quite a fuss, saying, 'Well, Tom, what a contrast, I only wish the weather was summer. You have made the *Aerolite* a home away from home. Everyone happy and contented. Now I realise what makes yachting, and to like yachting.'

Then his wife spoke, 'Tom,' she said, 'I expect you used to say a lot and bless us under your breath, when we crewed on *Harkaway*, done wrong and lost you a first prize.'

'Well, madam,' says I, 'you would be greatly shocked if you could hear it sometimes, but that is all in the work.'

So that ended 1931 and the learning how to sail the *Harkaway*.

* * *

In 1932, we fitted the *Aerolite* out and *Harkaway* as well and went through the same work of cruising around inside the Isle of Wight, but we raced more in the *Harkaway*. Sometimes when the boss left us, he would lend me and the *Harkaway* to a gentleman called Mr Gill. He was a designer of yachts and a very good helmsman. Anyway when he sailed *Harkaway*, we would get one of the three prizes given to our class for the three first boats of the race, but mostly the first prize. This year in between the races for *Harkaway* we would do a spot of line fishing from the *Aerolite*. The boss always asked me to put him where there would be plenty of fish. I done my best and we had some very good sport fishing with line. Sometimes we would anchor off Wootton. There we got the push nets out and in the early morning when the tide served for us, we would turn out at 5 o'clock, have a cup of tea and then I would take the boss and some of his guests in the launch and get some prawns and a good appetite for breakfast. This year we won nine prizes with *Harkaway*, six first, two seconds and one third. I thought that was not so bad, for our own crew of girls what we had trained was not always with us; then we would have a fresh crew and we had to make the best of them, learning them how we could in a race. The boss used to say, 'You don't mind do you, Tom? I only do it for sport and you seem to enjoy it.'

'Yes, sir,' I said, 'but it comes rather hard when you are first boat, then one of the crew gets tangled in the ropes and makes us lose first place. But now I have got used to it and when we lose our place of winning a prize after getting the boat in a position to win, I just say something and then that would happen now; it is all in the summer's work.'

17
Old Age

good gracious Tom what a splendid Picture of the Harkaway of there Why its worked in silk who done it Tom I replied I did and has a parting gift to you Sir for the Happy Time I have had in sereving you

Well this kind of life went on year in and year out till the year 1936. My wife had been attending the Eye Hospital for some time, then she went totally blind and her health was getting worse all the time. She was under the doctor's hands. We had sold the *Aerolite* and had only *Harkaway* to look after and we had laid her up at White's Yard, so it would be handy to my home for me to look after her and the store with a lot of the boss's personal gear.

I got out of bed one morning in October and went out for the count by collapsing on the floor. After a time I came to and my wife wanted me to stop home for the day and see a doctor, but I would not listen. I went to White's Yard, but not to work. In the meantime the doctor saw my dear wife and she told him all about me. He said to her, 'Tell him to be sure to come to me as soon as he gets home.'

So not feeling too good, I went to him. He had a fresh assistant come the same evening. After the doctor had run the rule over me, he told his mate to do the same. Then they both asked me what kind of work I done. I told him now that we had sold the large yacht

Tom and Fanny in their old age.

and only had the small yacht, I had to sail her myself from place to place wherever there was a race for her. Well, they both said I could not do it. If I attempted to do it again, the yacht would come back without me or as a dead man. I was not to do any more work. In fact I was not to do the slightest thing and rest all I could especially to lay down for an hour or two after the mid-day meal. So of course I went home and told my wife who had taken to her bed, as the doctor told me, for good, as old age was creeping on her fast, and me turning like I did, it was a sorrowful day for the both of us.

'I suppose it is God's will be done and that we must put our trust in Him,' was my dear wife's words to me.

I sat down then and wrote to my boss, that I should like to see him at White's Yard store urgently and as soon as possible. He came over on receiving my letter and he listened while I told him what the doctor had told me. He said, 'Well, Tom, I am more than sorry you won't be able to go sailing any more. You can just keep an eye on Harkaway and the store, and if you should want anything done, get the yard's men to do it while you look on; and, Tom, I shall want a man in your place; and I put it as a personal opinion to you that I will not take a man on, only by your own recommendation of him to me, and I only hope he will prove as good as you towards me, but there is a doubt in it.'

'But, sir,' I said, 'thanking you for the compliments, where there is one good man, sir, you will always find another.'

'Well, Tom,' he said, 'you have till the 1st of next May for to have the Harkaway ready to hand over to me and the new skipper you recommend. Mind though, no work. Let the yard do it.'

* * *

Well instead of keeping the Harkaway at White's we took her to Hamble and hauled her up there for the winter. I wrote to a chap

I knew at East Cowes after asking two of my own townsmen, and in March, 1937, he came over to Southampton. I took him to the boss's office in 11 London Road, Southampton, shipped him and put him on a retainer till the 15th April, when he was to take charge of her. On the 1st of May when we hoisted the burgee, so as we finished getting the boat off and on her moorings and ready the last of April, the boss called at my home in Poole Road, Itchen, took me to Warsash off which we had moorings, and had placed her on them. So on arriving at Warsash, Oatley (that was the name of the new skipper) took her over. The boss then said, 'Tom, this is a bad day for you. It is as the saying goes, "the end of your active career"; and I can only add I am as good as losing my right hand and may you live to a good age yet by taking things easy. You have only to let me know if you want anything and as long as it lays in my power, you shall have it.'

So by this time we had reached the shore and his car, I whispered to the motor man to pass my parcel to me. So taking the cover off it, I asked the boss if he would look at it.

'Good gracious, Tom, what a splendid picture of the *Harkaway*. Why it's worked in silk. Who done it, Tom?'

I replied, 'I did and as a parting gift to you, sir, for the happy time I have had in serving you. I have never had a better master in all my career.'

'Well, Tom, I shall always think of you when I see it. I will hang it in my hall and have it flood-lighted at night time so that all my guests can have a good view of it.'

So he took me home in his car, wished me all the best and I should have a turkey every Christmas he could get one. I have never seen him since, although I am receiving a gratuity ever since.

I took it very steady till 1939, with rumours of war and my wife sinking and wasting away. Bed-ridden and blind,

The silk picture of *Harkaway* that Tom made.

she passed away peacefully at 6pm on September 2nd, 1939. Those that has loved and lost, knows the meaning of 'gone,' and I know that. Well on the 3rd of September we declared war on Germany. So after putting my dear wife to her last resting place, I broke my home up and went and made my home with

156

my daughter Violet and her husband Charles Dickinson, and I could not have done better.

He was the first to offer me a home and I should have been happy all this last eight years but for one man – that madman Hitler. He properly upset all our apple-carts, for I think on the whole we had as much bombing from his 'planes in the sky as anyone. We had some very narrow shaves. A friend of our family had his own family in their own shelter one night when he gave us a really hard bombing. This friend's shelter had a direct hit with a bomb. The whole lot was finished. Well everyone around this district was expecting the same. A funny and lucky thing was my own family; I have five brothers and one sister all around this district; only the sister's house was tumbled down on top of them. No one was killed at the time, but her husband died later. They said that helped his death.

Now at this time my own family living was two sons, four daughters and their husbands, 25 grandchildren and five great-grandchildren. Not a bad family. I hope I shall live a few years yet to enjoy their company, and our country pull through this bad crisis. I have faith that we shall pull through that with the help of the One above.

My boss has passed on. The King had conferred the order of Knighthood in the New Year's Honour List about eight months before his death. But he remembered me till the last, and I greatly honour his memory. It was at this time that I had trouble with my strangulated hernia and I felt very queer, and I began to feel my age of 81 years. On calling my son-in-law one morning I gave a cough and my inside tumbled down. I felt I was finished for good; I tried to put it back in place, then I felt my stomach take a twist and oh! the agony of its pain! I stood it for two days,

The family at the wedding of Tom's daughter, Helena,
5 March 1927, Southampton.

then I had the doctor. He said I should have to go to the hospital, the only chance for me. My daughter said, 'Don't take him away, doctor.'

But the doctor said, 'Would you sooner see him lay there and die in less than 24 hours?'

I said, 'I will take the chance and go,' and so they rushed me to the hospital at 10.15pm. The ambulance men jammed my leg very badly, I have a bad leg now six weeks after it happened, but the operation was successful and I feel like a new man, with no pain and I feel I shall live a few years longer, the good Lord willing it so.

So I must hurry up now and finish my bit of a log of my life. I was 80 years old on August 20th, still my eyesight is good. I am writing this on Thursday, 2nd October, 1947.

So I will end this story of my life, trusting that anyone reading it will believe it is true as I remember it. I will conclude with my name.

So I will end this story of my live Trusting that anyone reading it will believe it is true has I remember it I will conclude with my name

Signed Thomas Diaper

Publishers' note:

Tom Diaper's Logbook was completed on 2 October 1947 and it was dedicated to his grand-daughter, Doreen Dickinson. Tom Diaper did not live to see the publication of his book; he died at the home of his daughter in Bitterne, Southampton, on 12 December 1949, at the age of 82.

Endnotes

Chapter 1

1 His father was Thomas 'Dutch' Diaper (1839–1902). He and his wife, Eliza Lonnon (1840–1922) married in 1860. They had six sons: Thomas (1867–1949); John Henry (1869–1957); Alfred William (1871–1950); Walter 'Mick' (1874–1952); Arthur Frederick (1876–1949) and Bertram Edward (1878–1949), and four daughters: Eliza Elizabeth (1865–1921); Ada Beatrice (1873–1937), Ethel Florence (1880–1881, died in infancy) and Evelyn Grace (1884–1962).

2 *Norman* (1872), composite cutter, 42 tons TM 61.8ft OA, 12.7ft beam. A 40-tonner cutter designed and built by Dan Hatcher, Southampton for Major William Ewing. Dutch Diaper was her skipper throughout Major Ewing's ownership, until she was put up for sale. During that period she won over 100 prizes. She was his most successful command. In 1882 she was bought by Lord Thomas Brassey.

3 *Niobe* (1863), 41 tons TM, 59ft OA, 12.9ft beam. Designed and built by Dan Hatcher, Southampton and owned by H Crawford. She was Dutch Diaper's first command, taking over on the death of his father, also called Thomas Diaper (1816–1863).

4 *Destiny* (1848), 83 tons TM, 91.8ft OA, 17.5ft beam. A two-masted schooner designed and built by William Camper at Gosport. In 1863 she was owned by Lt Col RC Grimes. She appears to have been used primarily for cruising and was unsuccessful as a racer.

5 It was William Gordon of Gordon Brothers, sail makers, High Street, Southampton, who is credited with designing the first spinnaker, which was recorded as being used, for the first time, on *Niobe*, on 5 June 1865. He did so at the request of Dutch Diaper, who wanted a sail that would give him a similar performance as he enjoyed when booming out a big jib sail on his fishing boat. The following year the new sail was adopted by the yacht *Sphinx* and the word 'spinnaker' appeared in a match report written by Dixon Kemp for *The Field* magazine.

6 *Christabel* (1858), racing cutter, 28 tons TM, 65.5ft OA, 12.0ft beam. Designed by R Aldous and built by Aldous, Brightlingsea. She was owned by Col Gourley.

7 It was his sister Eliza who let his brother, John Henry, fall into the stove. This must have happened in early 1870.

8 *Sleuth Hound* (1881), 40 tons TM, 64.0ft OA, 12.0ft beam. Cutter yacht designed and built by William Fife, Fairlie for the Marquis of Ailsa. Dutch Diaper was her skipper for two years, when she won the Queen's Cup at Cowes in 1882 and 1883.

9 *Annasona* (1881), 43 tons TM, 64.0ft OA, 12.0ft beam. Cutter yacht designed and built by William Fife, Fairlie for JBD Hedderwick. *Annasona* and *Sleuth Hound* were sister ships, although *Annasona*, under the command of William O'Neill, was the more successful of the two.

10 SY *Queen of Palmyra* (1876), 271 tons TM, 133.1ft OA, 21.3ft beam. Three masts. Designed and built by AE Payne & Sons, Southampton.

11 Records in the National Archives at Kew reveal that the *Queen of Palmyra*'s cook's boy, Abraham Collins of Tollesbury, drowned on 9 March 1882.

12 HMS *Alexandra* (1869), built at Chatham. 9,450 tons TM, 325ft OA. Two 11" guns and ten 10" guns. She had two central batteries, the upper mounted four 22-ton breach-loading guns and the lower eight 18-ton muzzle loaders, a combination of heavy armament not found in any other British battleship of the time. In 1882 she was the flagship of the fleet of 15 naval ships that were dispatched to bombard Alexandria in Egypt following a dispute that had its origins in a row between an Egyptian donkey boy and a Maltese man. This lead to anti-European riots in which several hundreds died, including 50 foreigners. The British demanded that the Khedive remove the heavy guns that defended the port. Their ultimatum was rejected and the ensuing bombardment, on 11 July 1882, lasted 10½ hours, at which point the Khedive decided to agree to Britain's request.

13 Referring to the yard of Alfred Payne & Sons, Southampton, the largest yacht yard in the area, at that time.

Chapter 2

1 SS *Asiatic* (1881), 2,087 gross, 299.9 X 34.2. A Cape cargo boat built by the Whitehaven Ship Building Company, Whitehaven for the Union

Steamship Company. A six-month voyage. *Asiatic* was subsequently lost in Mossel Bay, South Africa in April 1884.

2 SY *Dobhran* (1876), 440 tons TM, 193.0ft OA, 22.0ft beam. Built by Cunliffe & Dunlop, Port Glasgow. In 1884 she was owned by Thomas Valentine Smith.

3 SS *Athenian* (1881), 3,877 gross, 365 X 45.8. Built by Aitken & Mansel, Glasgow for the Union Steamship Company.

4 *Marguerite* (1884), 63 tons TM, 78.0ft OA, 13.6ft beam. A 60-tonner cutter designed by Alexander Richardson and built by Inman & Co, Lymington for Foster Connor of Belfast. In her first season she won only two first prizes out of 19 races. In 1885 Connor issued a challenge for the America's Cup. Although a yacht was designed by GL Watson, he sadly died of typhoid that same year before she could be built.

5 *Ileen* (1883), 29.84-ton cutter. 79.9ft OA, 11.4ft beam. Designed by John Harvey and built by Henry Piepgras, Greenport, New York. Her owner was Arthur Padelford, of New York. Arthur and his brother, Edward, were two of the most enthusiastic 'cutter-cranks' (those US yachtsmen who favoured yachts built to the British deep-keel, narrow-hull design, as opposed to the American national type, which was a broad-beamed, shallow-keeled centre boarder). Between 1883 and 1885 she was the second-largest cutter in US waters. Her skipper was Dutch Diaper, with an Itchen Ferry crew of seven.

6 *Ulidia* (1883), a ten-tonner cutter. 45.4ft OA, 7.2ft beam. Designed and built by William Fife, Fairlie. In 1886 she was brought from Scotland to New York by her new American owner, Edward Padelford.

7 In the 1887 season *Ileen's* main competition came from a new centre boarder, *Anaconda*, 56ft OA, 18.4ft beam, designed by Phil Elsworth of Bayonne and built by Poillion Brothers, Brooklyn.

8 SS *Servia* (1881), built by J & G Thomson, Glasgow for Cunard. 7,391 gross. 515ft OA, 52.1ft beam. 2 funnels, three masts rigged for sail. At the time of her launch she was the largest ship in the world, the first to be built from Siemens mild steel, the first to have electric light and Cunard's first double-bottomed ship. She was on the Liverpool/New York service.

9 *Thistle* (1887), 170 tons TM, 108.6ft OA, 20.3ft beam. Racing cutter. Designed by GL Watson and built by D & W Henderson, Glasgow for the James Bell Syndicate. *Thistle* was the British Challenger for the America's

Cup in 1887. She was defeated by the American defender *Volunteer*, designed by Edward Burgess. On her return to Britain she was modified and became a successful racer. In 1892 she was sold to the Kaiser who bought her to encourage his people to get involved with yachting and therefore incite a love of the sea and support for the German Navy.

10 On 7–8 October 1887 *Ulidia* raced the American sloop *Fanita*, also designed by Phil Elsworth, in a private match, for a US$500 cup, from the Larchmont Yacht Club, then based at New Rochelle, around Long Island to the Sandy Hook Lightship. *Fanita's* time was 34 hours 23 minutes and *Ulidia's* was 38 hours 34 minutes 30 seconds. Tom gives the margin as one hour!

11 SS *Etruria* (1884), built by John Elder & Co, Govan for Cunard. 8,128 gross, 519ft OA, 57.2ft beam. 19 knots. Two funnels, three masts rigged for sail. She was on the Liverpool/New York run. In March 1887 she took the record for the journey from Queenstown to Sandy Hook. Her best trip was 6 days 1 hour 55 minutes.

12 *Irex* (1884), 88 tons TM, 88.0ft OA, 15.1ft beam. A composite cutter designed by Alexander Richardson and built by JG Fay, Southampton. She belonged to John Jameson of the Jameson whiskey family of Dublin. Her captain was William O'Neill, one of the greatest of the Victorian yacht skippers. His autobiography was published as *A Yacht Master's Racing Record* in 1895.

13 On 17 August 1888, in the Royal Victoria Yacht Club race around the Isle of Wight, *Irex* smashed the course record, set by herself in 1886, with a time of 4 hours 50 minutes 41 seconds, in a fine-reaching wind. However Tom exaggerates their success in the Solent races that year, when the top yacht in her class was *Yarana*.

Chapter 3

1 *Valkyrie* (I) (1889), 94 tons TM, 85.0ft OA, 16.0ft beam. A composite racing cutter designed by GL Watson and built by JG Fay & Son, Southampton for the Earl of Dunraven. *Valkyrie* was ordered by Dunraven as a challenger for the America's Cup. However, the actual challenge fell through because the Royal Yacht Squadron as the Challenging Club could not agree the terms of the revised Deed of Gift that would govern how the matches would be fought. She proved to be a successful racer in British waters. Prior to

skippering *Valkyrie* (I), Dutch Diaper had commanded Lord Dunraven's first big racer, the cutter *Petronilla* (1888), 85 tons TM, 72.25ft OA, 17.0ft beam and designed by Alexander Richardson.

Valkyrie and *Irex* only raced against each other during the 1889 season.

In the spring of 1892 she was sold to Archduke Karl Stephen of Austria, once she had completed the Riviera season. She was eventually broken up in Gosport in 1904.

2 One can sense O'Neill's frustration. By the time of the Royal Clyde Regatta, on 6 July 1887, Dutch Diaper in *Valkyrie* had beaten *Irex* in ten of their 13 encounters that season. O'Neill's win that day must have been a much-needed boost to their fortunes. By the end of the season the score was 21:9 in favour of *Valkyrie*.

3 William G Jameson was John Jameson's brother. He was widely regarded as the finest amateur helmsman of his generation. Ben Parker would go on to be a famous yacht skipper himself.

4 *Mimosa* (1889), 28 tons TM, 55.8ft OA, 10.8ft beam. Designed by CP Clayton and built by W White & Sons, Cowes. Then owned by RH Cox.

5 SS *Nubia* (1882), built by D & W Henderson, Glasgow for Anchor Line. 3,551 gross, 378.2ft OA, 40.2ft beam. 12 knots. She was on the Glasgow/Liverpool/Bombay or Calcutta run. In January 1889 she sailed from Calcutta to Port Said to New York and Singapore. She sank off Brazil in 1911.

6 The largest cutters carried two mastheads men. Theirs was the most dangerous work on board, often involving having to climb up to 180 foot above a pitching deck. They were responsible for ensuring that sails and topsail yards did not snag on any part of the rigging while they were being hoisted or lowered. They were also responsible for lacing the luff of the topsail to the topmast. Both positions were the established routes for someone to be appointed as a mate. It was work only for the smartest hands. The dangers attaching to both positions were recognised by extra daily pay.

On a large cutter the end of the bowsprit could extend 40 foot in front of the bow. The bowsprit-ends man had to help with the setting and taking down of the huge jibs. It required a keen sense of balance, the work being uncomfortable and very wet.

7 *Alwida* (1890), 9 tons TM, 33.0ft OA, 8.4ft beam. A five-rater racing cutter designed by AE Payne and built by A Payne & Son, Southampton for

Lord Dunraven. In her 1891 season she took part in 40 races and won 14 and had 16 places (Tom gives us her results while he was on board from early August 1890).

8   The Brambles is a well-known shoal of the Solent, between Calshot and Cowes.

9   Both Watson and Dutch Diaper wished to be responsible for the fitting out of *Valkyrie*. Watson had a very fine reputation for ensuring that no back-handers were taken from yards or suppliers during the fitting-out process. He was always anxious to ensure that the owner got best value for money, and naturally enough Watson would have been paid for arranging and inspecting the fitting out. We can only speculate that Dutch felt that he was being done out of one of the perks of the job, because he would not be able to receive such payments.

Dutch's stand on this is strange because he must have known that he would have been appointed as skipper on the recommendation of Watson. To have 'crossed' Watson was not a great career move!

10   *Mischief* (1873), 19 tons TM, 42.0ft OA, 12.4ft beam. A ten-rater racing cutter. Built by McCabe, Lough Erne to the design of Lt Henry Gartside Tipping RN, her owner of Kingstown, Ireland. *Mischief* was a remarkably fast vessel. The shallow waters of upper Lough Erne had encouraged the development of a shallow-bodied, broad-beamed boat carrying a centre board (very similar to the American national type), quite unlike the deep-bodied, narrow-beamed cutter exemplified by *Doris*, Watson's champion ten-rater, whom she defeated in a series of match races at the Kingstown Regatta in 1887. Prior to those races her centreboard was removed, as they were barred by the RYA rules, and she was fitted with a thin metal keel with a bulb of lead weighing 5 tons, a design development that would be much copied.

11   Tipping was responsible for surveying all the RNLI lifeboats on the Irish Coast, Isle of Man and the West Coast of England from the Solway down to Caernarvon (70 stations). This was a huge area to cover and, at that time, with difficult communications. He had her altered to become a 27-ton sea-going cruiser and used her to travel between the lifeboat stations. As he sailed from port to port he took part in local regattas as the opportunity arose. She was an excellent and safe seaboat.

12 On 7 November 1890 Tom Diaper married Fanny Trayhorn (1870–
    1939). They had two boys and six girls, including Fanny who died in
    the 1918 flu epidemic.

Chapter 4

1 *Maid Marion* (ex *Yarana*) (1888), 72 tons TM, 75.8ft OA, 14.9ft beam.
   A 65-rater cutter designed by GL Watson and built by D & W Henderson.
   She was then owned by Myles B Kennedy.

2 In the 1891 season, *Maid Marion* raced 19 times but only got one first and one
   place. So Tom would have received very little much-needed prize money.
   She had her last race that season on 19 August. In the 1892s she had 17
   races and won two races with one other place (hardly a lot of prizes as
   Tom suggests). In the 1893 season she only entered one race on 1 August,
   coming in second. Tom's move to *Navahoe* was aimed at earning more prize
   money. As noted below, that boat proved to be no more successful.

3 HMS *Trincomalee* (1817), built in Bombay as a 6th rating frigate. At the
   time Diaper is referring to she was being used as a reserve training ship
   in Southampton.

4 SS *Scot* (1890), 6,844 gross, 500ft OA, 54.7ft beam. 18.5 knots. Built
   by William Denny & Brothers, Dumbarton for the Union Line. She had
   two masts. She was the first twin-screw steamer used on the run to the
   Cape of Good Hope. She had been built as a record breaker regardless
   of cost. In March 1893 she made a record run of 14 days 18 hours 57
   minutes, which remained unbroken for 43 years.

5 *Navahoe* (1893), 113.2 tons TM, 126.0ft OA, 23.0ft beam. A composite
   sloop designed and built by Herreshoff & Co, Bristol, Rhode Island for
   Royal Phelps Carroll of New York. She was designed as a cruiser-racer
   and therefore was somewhat less formidable as a racer than the typical
   Herreshoff product.

   In UK waters in 1893 she took part in 18 races and won two with
   three places. She lost in all 13 of her races with *Britannia*. Dutch Diaper
   was her pilot throughout her time in British waters. He repeated that
   role when the big American sloop, *Vigilant*, came over the following year.

6 *Britannia* (1893), 221 tons TM, 100.0ft OA, 23.3ft beam. A composite
   cutter designed by GL Watson and built by D & W Henderson for the
   Prince of Wales. She set 10,327sq ft of sail.

7 *Valkyrie II* (1893), 191 TM 117.3 OA 22.4 beam. A composite cutter designed by GL Watson and built by D & W Henderson for the Earl of Dunraven. She set 10,271sq ft of sail. She was Dunraven's second attempt at the America's Cup. In 1893 she met *Vigilant*, the American defender, and was defeated in three straight races.

8 *Satantia* (1893), 300 tons TM, 117.1ft OA, 24.7ft beam. A composite cutter designed by JM Soper and built by JG Fay & Son, Southampton for AD Clarke. She set 9,923sq ft of sail. She was the fastest-ever cutter on a broad reach, making 17 knots. However, she was comparatively unsuccessful as a racer as she lacked manoeuvrability.

9 *Calluna* (1893), 258 tons TM, 106.6ft OA, 24.3ft beam. A composite cutter designed by William Fife and built by A & J Inglis, Glasgow for Peter Donaldson of Glasgow. She proved to be a complete failure and this pretty well put paid to Fife's hopes of breaking into designing yachts for the Big Class.

10 Diaper is describing the race for the Breton Reef Cup, which took place on 14 September 1893. It was one of the finest and most dramatic yacht races of the Victorian era.

11 *Genesta* (1884), 80 tons TM, 96.5ft OA, 15.0ft beam. A composite cutter designed by J Beavor-Webb and built by D & W Henderson as Sir Richard Gordon's challenger for the America's Cup in 1885. She was defeated by *Puritan*, designed by Edward Burgess.

12 *Galatea* (1885), 90 tons TM, 102.7ft OA, 15.0ft beam. A composite cutter designed by J Beavor-Webb and built by J Reid & Co, Port Glasgow. She was Lt William Henn's challenger for the America's Cup in 1886 when she was roundly defeated by *Mayflower*, designed by Edward Burgess. She was really built as a cruiser and Henn's chances of success had been a mere pipe dream.

13 The reason for the threatened strike was that the crew wanted to receive their prize money, rather than any desire to ensure that *Navahoe* was credited with winning the race. The owner presumably had been reticent about protesting the Prince of Wales.

14 *Ellen* (1894), 44 tons TM, 55.8ft OA, 14.13ft beam. Twenty-rater cutter designed by GL Watson and built by J Adam, Gourock for Count William Douglas. Douglas was a descendant of the 'Black Douglases'

who had been forced into exile from Scotland many centuries earlier. He owned an extensive estate on Rügen, a German Island in the Baltic.

15 The voyage described took in Sassnitz on the seaward side of Rügen, Travemünde, the most south-westerly German port on the Baltic and Swinemünde, which lies close to Stettin on the Baltic.

16 In the early 1890s Douglas started to landscape his grounds and it is clear from what Tom Diaper writes that Douglas endeavoured to encourage the crew of his yacht to form part of his work detail. This led to the Germans in his crew walking out as a result of an early example of a demarcation dispute as to what was to be expected of a yacht crew and what was not.

17 Stralsund is the largest port on the Island of Rügen and faces the German mainland.

18 *Vigilant* (1893), 144.77 tons TM, 124.0ft OA, 26.4ft beam. Designed and built by Herreshoff & Co, Bristol, Rhode Island for the Oliver Iselin Syndicate. She successfully defended the America's Cup against the *Valkyrie* II challenge of 1893. Her arrival to race in British waters in 1894 caused a very considerable stir, since she was an out and out racer, unlike *Navahoe* of the previous season. Her sail area was 10,042sq ft. She was defeated by *Britannia* in 11 out of their 17 races together in UK waters that year.

19 Tom was watching the collision between *Valkyrie* and *Satanita* from some 3½ miles distance, on the far side of the Clyde Estuary on a day with poor visibility. Both yachts were part of a fleet of the Big Class all heading for the start line at the Mudhook Regatta. A small lugsail boat with five men aboard suddenly appeared in the path of *Satanita*. *Satanita* had to luff up sharply to avoid an immediate collision with the men. As it was she dismasted the small boat. The captain and helmsman struggled to get *Satanita* off the wind, but even with full rudder she did not respond. As she was travelling at top speed she was unable to avoid a collision with *Valkyrie II*, striking her hard amidships. Just before the collision the mastheadmen on *Valkyrie* started to slide down the shrouds, but the force of the collision threw them into the water. The two vessels, locked together, drifted down on to a steam yacht moored at the start line. Small boats were quickly launched to pick up Dunraven, his female

guests and GL Watson, who was on board that day. *Valkyrie's* crew of 37 mainly jumped overboard. Unusually they were all swimmers and they trod water watching their boat, with all their possessions, sink. The only casualty was a member of her crew who was crushed to death, having fallen between the sinking yacht and the steam yacht. It was remarkable that more did not die.

Chapter 5

1 SS *Victoria* (1887), 6,522 gross, 465.8ft OA, 52.0ft beam. Built by Caird & Co, Greenock for P & O. She was single screw with four masts. She sailed between the UK and India and the UK and Australia. With her three sister ships, she was the fastest and most expensive liner in the P & O fleet. The passage to Bombay would have taken her 12½ days.

2 *L'Esperance* (1891), 76 tons TM, 75.8ft OA, 15.4ft beam. Designed by AE Payne as a fast cruiser, she was built by Camper & Nicholson, Gosport for Lord Dunraven. Dunraven sold her in August 1895 and she passed to Prince Henry of Prussia, the Kaiser's brother. Dunraven was still racing her at the end of 1893. She was broken up in 1913–1914.

3 *Audrey* (1894), 20 tons TM, 65.28ft OA, 13.15ft beam. She was originally designed by Lord Dunraven (with some help from GL Watson) but was a complete failure in her first season of 1894. Dunraven called in Watson who re-designed her completely below the waterline, after which she was successful. She was built (and rebuilt in 1895), by Summers & Payne, Southampton. She was further significantly modified in 1896, by which time very little of the original boat was left.

4 *Niagara* (1895), sloop, 65.0ft OA, 12.0ft beam. She was built by Herreshoff for the American, Howard Gould. (Tom's memory has slightly failed, in fact by the time *Audrey* and *Niagara* reached Southampton in 1895, the score is 3:2 in favour of *Niagara*. By the end of that season they would tie 6 all.)

Chapter 6

1 *Isolde* (1895), 82 tons TM, 71.25ft OA, 16.8ft beam. A composite cutter designed and built by William Fife, Fairlie originally for Peter Donaldson. The accident to *Isolde* killed her owner Baron von Zedwitz.

2 *Meteor* (II) (1896), 238 tons TM, 100.0ft OA, 24.3ft beam. Designed by GL Watson and built by D & W Henderson, Glasgow for the Kaiser. The Kaiser had ordered a new boat from Watson with the specific intention of defeating the Prince of Wales' *Britannia*. Watson duly obliged with an enlarged version of *Britannia*. It is interesting to note that the British–German naval rivalry had spilled over into yachting. Her last season racing in UK waters was 1897.

3 *Audrey* had been in commission throughout the 1896 season. Up to the date of the *Isolde* dismasting, *Audrey* had beaten her that season nine times to *Isolde*'s five. So why Dunraven replaced his crew with that of *Isolde*'s is unclear. When *Audrey* went down to the West Country the record shows that she got two firsts at Torbay and one second; a first and a second at Dartmouth, a first at Start Bay, and four seconds at Plymouth.

4 *Meteor* did not race in the handicap class and therefore the only competition she had in 1897 in English waters was *Caress* (1895), 78 tons TM, 70.5ft OA, 16.5ft beam, a 60-rater composite cutter designed by GL Watson and built by D & W Henderson, Glasgow. The new YRA time allowance system for that season severely penalised *Meteor*.

5 The unreasonable time penalty imposed on *Meteor* in the 1897 season was the reason why the Kaiser decided in 1898 that she would not race in English waters that year. She only raced at Kiel in 1898, hence the reason why Tom was paid off.

6 *Marolga* (1898), 35 tons TM, 60.8ft OA, 11.5ft beam. Designed by Max Oertz and built by Max Oertz & Harder, Hamburg for A Hasenclever and F Ewers of Lübeck.

7 *Klein Polly* (1899), 8 tons TM, 36.0ft OA, 7.3ft beam. Designed by Max Oertz and built by Max Oertz & Harder, Hamburg for GW Büxenstein. She was sloop rigged.

8 *Polly* (1899), 30 tons TM, 59.7ft OA, 10.7ft beam. Designed by Max Oertz and built by Max Oertz & Harder, Hamburg for GW Büxenstein, Berlin. She was cutter rigged.

Chapter 8

1 SS *Canada* (1896). Built by Harland & Wolff, Belfast for the Dominion Line. 8,800 gross, 500ft OA, 58.2ft beam. 15 knots. She was the first

twin-screw steamship on the Canadian service. Her main trips were Liverpool, Quebec and Montreal, but on occasions she went to New York. She was used as a troop ship to South Africa from November 1899 to late 1902.

2 Virginia II (1899) (originally called Oiseau), 43.0ft OA, 10.0ft beam. Designed and built by Herreshoff, Bristol, Rhode Island as a knockabout. At that time she belonged to Isaac Stern of New York.

3 SY Virginia (1899), 442 tons TM, 199.5ft OA, 25.8ft beam. Designed by GL Watson and built by the Bath Iron Works, Maine for Isaac Stern.

4 Iduna (1887) (originally called Yampa), 364 tons TM, 121.0ft OA, 27.0ft beam. Designed by A Cary Smith and built by Horlan & Hollingsworth, Wilmington, Delaware. At the time referred to she was owned by the German Empress.

Chapter 9

1 Iris (1874), yawl, 57 tons TM, 62.2ft OA, 15.1ft beam. Designed and built by Alfred Burlace, Plymouth and owned by J Conway Lloyd of Brecon, South Wales.

2 Vesta (1900), yawl, 51 tons TM, 68.9ft OA, 13.1ft beam. Built by DW Kremersohn, Elmshom and owned by GW Büxenstein, Berlin. Quite why the Kaiser 'ordered' Büxenstein to cruise around the Mediterranean is unclear.

3 Iris (1903), 48-ton cutter, 66.0ft OA, 13.0ft beam. Designed by G Borg and built by Neptun Werft, Rostock. She was owned by Capt-Lieut Mischke of Keil.

4 Hubertus (1903), 32 tons TM cutter, 47.5ft WL, 13.3ft beam. Designed by Max Oertz and built by Max Oertz Yachtwerft, Hamburg. She was owned by A Gossmann and H Behnecke.

5 Carola (1905), yawl, 41 tons TM, 56.7ft OA, 13.4ft beam. Designed by Max Oertz and built by Max Oertz Yachtwerft, Hamburg. She was owned by Capt L Weidle, Hamburg.

6 Kranick (II) (1902), sloop, 12 tons TM, 42.0ft OA, 8.3ft beam. Designed by Max Oertz and built by Max Oertz Yachtwerft, Hamburg. Owned by Otto Mendelssohn-Bartholdy.

Chapter 10

1 SY *Sea Snake* (1876), 108 tons TM, 104.0ft OA, 15.1ft beam. Designed and built by J & G Thomson, Glasgow. Owned by Alexander Macdonald. (Presumably MacDonald had bought her with a view to reselling her.)

2 Alexander Macdonald & Co, Boat Builders, Ferry Yard, Elm Road (now Hazel Road), Itchen. The yard was on the east bank of the River Itchen, just upstream of the Itchen Bridge, Southampton.

3 SY *Kathlinda* (1877), 67 tons TM, 93.8ft OA, 12.65ft beam. Designed and built by J Reid & Co, Port Glasgow. Then owned by Lt CDJ Rafarel.

4 SY *Jason* (1877), 416 tons TM, 161.7ft OA, 23.7ft beam. Designed by J St Claire Byrne and built by the Barrow Ship Building Co. Owned by Frank Biddy.

5 *Witch* (1902), 8 tons TM, 30.6ft OA, 8.3ft beam. Designed and built by C Sibbick, Cowes. Then owned by CGA Burnett, London.

Chapter 11

1 The records of the RNLI show that on 12 March 1914 the Totland Lifeboat, the *Robert Fleming*, took one person off the 'dismasted' yacht *Coo-ee* of Southampton. Tom sailed to Yarmouth, being the closest port to enter in a westerly gale. This required him to pass through the Hurst Narrows, no small feat of seamanship in such a gale with big seas running. In 1914 the lifeboat station was based at Totland Bay and not at Yarmouth itself. The *Robert Fleming* was a 37-foot boat pulled by 12 oars. The Totland Bay lifeboat slip was very exposed to westerly gales, which sent heavy and confused seas over the Shambles Bank that lies opposite the lifeboat station, extending all the way back to the mainland along the western side of the westerly approach to the Solent.

2 SS *Cap Trafalgar* (1913), 18,710 tons, 590.4ft OA, 72.2ft beam. Triple expansion engines. Top speed 17 knots. 1,580 passengers, 330 crew. Built in Hamburg for the German Hamburg–South America Line. At the outbreak of the First World War she was converted to become an armed merchant cruiser. Two weeks after the war started she sailed from

Montevideo and then disguised herself as the Union Castle Line vessel, Carmania, having removed one of her three funnels. On 14 September 1914, by one of the ironies of war, the Carmania, also converted to an armed merchant cruiser, encountered the Cap Trafalgar off the coast of Brazil. After a 1 hour 40 minute battle the guns of the Carmania sank the Cap Trafalgar. This is the only time that two ocean liners have engaged each other in a duel.

3 SS Carmania (1905). Built by John Browns, Glasgow for Cunard. 9,524 gross, 650.4ft OA, 72.2ft beam. Two funnels two masts. Triple-screw 18 knots. Also see note above.

4 Nis (1900), yawl, 38 tons TM, 55.4ft OA, 12.9ft beam. Designed by A Muller and built by C Scharstein, Dietrichsdorf. She was owned by M Jebsen, Hamburg.

5 Tate's Navy – the popular name for the Royal Navy Patrol Service. In the First World War the Navy put together a fleet of hundreds of requisitioned trawlers, drifters, whalers, paddle steamers, yachts, tugs and other 'minor vessels of war' and armed them with obsolete weapons. They were used mainly for patrol, mine-sweeping and anti-submarine work. (Harry Tate was a pre-First World War music hall entertainer who played the part of a clumsy comic who could not get to grips with various contraptions. So the name 'Tate' came to mean anything clumsy and amateurish.)

6 SS Minnesota (1887), 3,216 gross, 345.5 X 40.9. Built by Harland & Wolf for the Atlantic Transport Line. One funnel two masts. 11 knots. Originally a cattle carrier. Then used as a troop transport. She was used on the Liverpool–Baltimore route.

Chapter 12

1 SS Imperator (1912) (later named Berengaria). Built by AG Vulcan, Hamburg. 52,226 gross, 883.5ft OA, 98.3ft beam. Three funnels two masts four propellers. She was powered by four turbines. 25 knots. At the end of the First World War she was seized as a war prize and handed over to Cunard, as a replacement for the Lusitania. They renamed her Berengaria, who used her for fast passages across the Atlantic. In 1919 she was used as a US troop transporter. She normally had a crew of 1,180 and carried 2,800 passengers.

Chapter 13

1 *Shamrock* (23-metre) (1908), cutter, 94.02 tons TM, 96.6ft OA, 20.85ft beam. Designed and built by William Fife & Son, Fairlie for Sir Thomas Lipton. She carried 9,843sq ft of sail. She sailed across the Atlantic, arriving in New York on 7 June 1920. She acted as the trial horse for *Shamrock IV*. She was skippered by Tom's brother Alf, along with Tom, three other brothers and two of Alf's sons. So out of a total crew of 22, seven were Diapers.

2 *Shamrock IV* (1914), 97.21 tons TM, 110.4ft OA, 24.0ft beam. Designed by Charles E Nicholson and built by Camper & Nicholson, Gosport for Sir Thomas Lipton. She carried 10,459sq ft of sail.

3 *Resolute* (1914), 99 tons TM, 106.4ft OA, 21.1ft beam. Designed and built by the Herreshoff Manufacturing Company, Bristol, Rhode Island. She carried 8,775sq ft of sail.

4 SS *Lapland* (1908), built by Harland & Wolff for the Red Star Line, Antwerp. 18,695 tons. 605.8ft OA, 70.4ft beam. 17 knots. Four masts two funnels. 370 crew, 1,430 passengers. Her usual run was Antwerp to New York, calling at Southampton. She was the largest ship to have sailed under the Belgium flag. The ship was not without glamour. On an earlier trip that year Douglas Fairbanks and Mary Pickford had honeymooned on board.

5 *Patience* (1894), cutter, 22 tons TM, 40.6ft OA, 12.0ft beam. Built by PT Harris, Rowhedge. Then owned by Melville Neill of Lochgilphead.

6 *Kate* (1861), cutter, 12 tons TM, 34.6ft OA, 9.6ft beam. Built by W Halliday, Cowes. Then owned by Richard Brereton of Rugby.

7 *Terpischore* (1920) (later known as *Lulworth*), 186 tons TM, 95.5ft long, 21.8ft beam. Designed by W White and built by White Brothers, Southampton. Owned by RM Lee.

Chapter 14

1 *Mollihawk* (1903), 28.8 tons TM aux schooner, 59.6ft long, 14.74ft beam. Designed by Linton Hope and built by Courtney & Birkett, Southwick. She carried 2,135sq ft of sail. She was owned by Eustace Pinkerton.

Pinkerton also owned the yawl, *Heartsease* (1898), 88 tons TM, 78.0ft OA, 16.4ft beam. Designed by AE Payne and built by Camper & Nicholson. He clearly valued his privacy as his address is given as c/o The Bank of Nova Scotia, Halifax.

2 Floating dock, Southampton. In 1924 an enormous floating dry dock was constructed by Armstrong Whitworth, Newcastle, to be based in Southampton to handle the three gigantic German war prizes: *Imperator*, *Vaterland* and *Bismark* (then renamed *Berengaria*, *Leviathan* and *Majestic*). It was large enough to accommodate the largest ship in the world, which was then the *Majestic* at 56,000 tons. It could handle ships of up to 60,000 tons and 960ft long. It was opened by the Prince of Wales on 24 June 1924. It first came into service on 27 June 1924.

3 *Florinda* (1873), a 135-ton yawl, 101.0ft OA, 19.2ft beam. Designed and built by Camper & Nicholson (now a house-boat). Like so many old racers she would have been stripped of her lead keel and sold off as a house-boat.

4 *Florinda II* (1920), a 26-ton twin-screw ketch. 52.5ft OA, 11.2ft beam. Built by H Heidtman, Hamburg. She was owned by WC Bersey of Princes Gate, London. To describe her as a launch is therefore slightly misleading but no doubt she was used in that role.

5 Charles Hatry was a company promoter and financier. Prior to the collapse of his empire it had been worth £24 million. A great many investors were ruined. Found guilty of forging bearer certificates, he was sentenced to 14 years in prison.

Chapter 15

1 MY *Aerolite* (1880) (formerly the steam tug *Garland*). 84 tons, 90.0ft OA, 15.1ft beam. Built by R Chambers & Co, Dumbarton. By 1930 she was powered by a paraffin engine. Owned by Commander James Bird RN (rtd). His principal residence was at the Grosvenor House, London.

2 *Harkaway* (1927), 34ft 6 inch OA, 24ft WL, 5ft 1" draft. A West Solent Restricted (or One Design) Class designed by HG May, in 1924, and built by the Berthon Boat Company, Lymington. 45ft mast. The design was initially commissioned by the Royal Lymington Yacht Club as a cruiser-racer. In 1927 such a boat cost £600 supplied fully rigged. Those built for the East Coast became known as the Royal Burnham Restricted Class.

Index